TELEWORKING IN THE COUNTRYSIDE

Teleworking in the Countryside

Home-based working in the information society

MICHAEL ANTONY CLARK
Countryside and Community Research Unit
Cheltenham and Gloucester College of Higher Education

Ashgate

Aldershot • Burlington USA • Singapore • Sydney

Published by
Ashgate Publishing Limited
Gower House
Croft Road
Aldershot
Hampshire GU11 3HR
England

Ashgate Publishing Company
131 Main Street
Burlington, VT 05401-5600 USA

Ashgate website: http://www.ashgate.com

British Library Cataloguing in Publication Data
Clark, Michael Antony
 Teleworking in the countryside : home-based working in the
 information society. - (Urban and regional planning and
 development)
 1.Telecommuting - Great Britain 2.Cottage industries -
 Great Britain
 I.Title
 331.2'5

Library of Congress Control Number: 00-134493

ISBN 0 7546 1061 6

Printed and bound in Great Britain, by Antony Rowe Ltd., Chippenham

Contents

PART 1
INTRODUCTION AND RESEARCH METHODOLOGY

PART 2
THE FACILITATION OF, AND DEMAND FOR, TELEWORK

List of Figures

List of Tables

Acknowledgements

A huge debt of gratitude is owed to the many individuals who were involved in the research project. I would especially like to thank all the teleworkers who gave up their time to help with the research and for providing such a fascinating, lucid and valuable insight into their lives. I am additionally grateful to all of the agencies and organisations who were willing to take part in the research project.

PART 1

Introduction and Research Methodology

1 Telework and the Changing Rural Economy

The economy of rural Britain has witnessed considerable restructuring in the post war period. Farming-related employment, the traditional base of the rural economy, has been in continuous decline being replaced by manufacturing and particularly service sector employment. Research into rural employment has tended to focus on the importance of manufacturing jobs throughout the 1980s and early 1990s, in part, engendered from a desire to explore a so called 'urban-rural manufacturing shift'.

However, it has been suggested that the impact of manufacturing growth in rural areas has been overstated and that the greatest increases in rural employment in recent years have been within the service sector, particularly amongst small businesses and self-employment (Cloke et al, 1997). Of particular interest has been the introduction of technology-led service jobs, plugged in to urban-based markets through the introduction of new information technologies into traditionally inaccessible places. Certainly, the development of information and communication technologies (ICT), along with shifts towards non-material production and information-based employment, have engendered considerable speculation as to how their integration may facilitate major shifts in the organisation of work:

> With the diffusion of computer network technology, an increasing share of economic activity in different regions will be mediated and integrated through advanced telecommunication systems. [This has enabled] the mediation of work tasks through computer networks [which] is commonly referred to as "teleworking" (Gillespie and Hepworth, 1988, p. 4).

Teleworking, along with many other labels such as distance working, telecottaging, telecommuting and electronic homeworking, has come to encompass a range of new work practices associated with a spatial re-organisation of employment. Essentially through the integration of information and communication technologies, (termed telematics), such as computers, modems, e-mail and the Internet, a range of information-based occupations have become spatially less constrained. This has enabled them to be performed in more flexible workspaces (such as the home), located outside more traditional workspaces such as the office within the city.

3

Since the 1970s, a wide range of academic, policy and popular literature has focused on the implications of, and opportunities facilitated through, telework and a possible shift of work out of the office and into the home. In many ways telework has been linked to a de-urbanisation of employment and a shift back to a pre-industrial landscape based on hi-tech homeworking in re-vitalised people and place-based communities in the countryside. Such visions have resulted in substantial speculation as to how rural areas may be recipients of these new working practices. This has been particularly so in the popular media, which has focused on the lifestyle opportunities created through telework, and also from policy makers who have viewed telework as a new tool for social and economic development in rural areas.

It is generally accepted that telework principally involves information or knowledge-based occupations in which work tasks can be processed and transmitted via telematics to employers or clients, from remote workspaces such as the home, satellite office or neighbourhood office. However, while there have been attempts to broaden the concept of telework, particularly in relation to the nature of the tele 'workspace' (for example, satellite offices), it has been teleworking from the home which has received the greatest attention from academics, policy makers and the popular media as it has represented the most radical and novel shift in the location of work.

Despite this considerable interest in home-based telework, many academic researchers have encountered definitional problems when attempting to select and locate home-based teleworkers to study. This has resulted in the development of a number of competing definitions rather than one generally agreed definition of telework. For example, telework has been defined as working at home for a significant proportion of working time, in order to exclude those who only make incidental use of a computer at home or who simply use the home as a base and as such should not be included in a definition of telework.

In addition, central to most interpretations of telework has been the use of information and communication technologies (ICT) to produce and communicate work to and from organisations. For instance, Cross and Raizman (1986) defined telework as performing job-related work at a site away from the office and then transferring the results electronically to the office or other locations. Huws (1993) stated that a teleworker should use both a computer device and telecommunications device in undertaking the work, as they would be unable to work at home without using this technology. However, one can question whether a person (for example a freelance journalist), becomes a 'teleworker' if s/he already works from home and simply upgrades from a typewriter to a computer. Given these arguments, it is important to recognise that teleworkers should not necessarily be characterised by their use of technology, but by the nature of their work, in that it involves the production and communication of information from home.

It is also important to recognise that limiting definitions to just those workers who use telecommunications technology to work at home might be too restrictive. As such, definitions of telework should be based on a broader conception of remote communication between the worker and client/employer. Examples of such working methods are where postal and courier services are used to send disks or hard copies to clients, and where the telephone is used to maintain effective contact with organisations.

While academics have based their research upon these broader conceptions of telework, they have still considered what appear to be a broad range of non-exclusive working practices as telework. More specifically, much of the research has focused on teleworking employees - working for a single employer and receiving all the pay and benefits as on site staff - as well as self-employed or freelance teleworkers - small businesses or independent contractors working for a variety of client organisations on a contract. However, while it has been noted that the motivations behind, and characteristics and experiences of, employed and self-employed telework differ considerably, researchers have tended to ignore this fact, often confusing the experience of telework with homeworking rather than contractual status. For example, Olson (1988) has indicated that:

> People who work at home work under a variety of conditions of employment. There has been considerable confusion caused by the tendency to generalise across different conditions. A greater problem has been the tendency to attribute abuses (or potential abuses) of workers to the fact that they are at home rather than to the conditions of their employment (p. 80).

It is therefore dangerous and ambiguous, to use telework as a label for such a variety of work practices simply on the basis that individuals use remote communications to work from home. After all, telework, as with 'office working', is simply a way of working and not a job per se. Indeed, Rawlins (1990) suggested 'you will never get advertisements saying "teleworker wanted"' (p. 5). Rather telework is a new method by which a range of information-based occupations can be undertaken. Ultimately, it can be questioned what these different work arrangements termed telework have in common and subsequently the extent to which telework forms an identifiable unit of measurement. Craipiau and Marot (1984), quoted by Cross and Burton (1993), suggested that 'a pluristical and monolithic definition of telework ... would ultimately be abstract and unrealistic' (p. 349). Subsequently they argued the existence of various degrees and types of telework such as that of self-employed and employee teleworkers. In addition, Huws et al (1990) suggested that:

> These many difficulties facing the researcher attempting to produce a clear definition of telework prompt the question, why bother? If a concept is as nebulous as this, then wouldn't it be better to abandon it and develop a different framework for analysis more amenable to precise categorisation? Perhaps instead of focusing on telework, we should be concentrating on a study of the changing geographical organisation of work, or new travel patterns, or the use of information technology by home-based workers, or new forms of contractual relationships between employers and workers, or of changing patterns of work organisation (p. 8).

Although in this statement, Huws et al (1990) advocate the rejection of telework as a useful analytical definition, it does appear that recent shifts towards more flexible forms of capitalist accumulation have given rise to particular, dominant forms of telework. More specifically, telework has been linked to organisational change, corporate rationalisation, increases in the levels of sub-contracting and the growth of flexible employment patterns such as self-employment. In particular, home-based telework can be linked to the growth in sub-contracting and the growth of self-employed individuals working from home. Moreover, it has been suggested that, while employed telework will increasingly address a declining part of the workforce (Mitchell 1995), the vast majority of homeworking individuals consist of independent self-employed contractors who have set up their own information-based business, which happens to be based at home (Olson, 1988).

Self-employed telework also appears to have the greatest relevance for rural areas. For instance, popular notions of telework, offered by a number of commentators, and seen in the popular literature, have focused on telework as representing a set of combined lifestyle and workstyle shifts - from living and working for an organisation in the city to living and working for oneself in the countryside. Moreover, whilst self-employment has long been a dominant form of employment in rural areas, self-employed telework can be seen as enabling those who already live in, or who have moved to the countryside previously, to engage in professional work not available locally. It can also be argued that only self-employed telework has the potential to develop substantially in rural areas due to its associated spatial, temporal and contractual freedoms. Employed teleworkers, on the other hand, are likely to have been employed by a teleworking employer for some time in a non-teleworking capacity and therefore would tend to be located within daily commuting distance of the organisation, usually in urban centres.

Much of the literature on rural teleworking has focused on the concept of the rural telecottage. The telecottage can be defined as a central resource centre, providing access to, and training in, ICT (for example, computers, e-mail, the Internet and faxes), aimed at helping those individuals wishing to start a teleworking business but without the necessary skills or equipment, supporting established teleworkers seeking a workspace outside of the home, and offering specialist training, advice and equipment. The growth of telecottages in rural areas can also be linked to the growth in sub-contracting and self-employment. For example, a central role of the telecottage has been seen to be as a 'telebureau' - a form of on-line employment bureau - importing work into the area from large, often remote, urban-based companies via ICT and then outsourcing the work on a contract basis to local, home or telecottage-based teleworkers. In many ways, therefore, telecottages rely predominantly on self-employed telework for their income, both in terms of the provision of services to self-employed workers, and also through the telebureau concept, engaging in a sub-contracting role themselves.

However, despite the possible spatial, cultural, social and economic implications of a possible annihilation of space inherent in the telework concept, much of the telework debate has been largely informed by anecdotal examples, journalistic reporting and individual forecasts. Presently, therefore, little is known about the nature, scale and experiences of telework in the countryside.

This book aims to redress the empirical imbalance by drawing upon a considerable amount of empirical evidence to present a critical, objective and rigorous analysis of telework from the perspective of individual teleworkers, policy makers and organisations based in, and around, two geographically contrasting rural case study areas, one located in rural Wales and the other in the South East of England. There are three key themes on which the research will focus. Firstly, it will explore the characteristics and dynamics of self-employed telework in rural areas, for example, the extent to which telework is locationally independent of client organisations and, as such, a potential rural activity facilitating rural in-migration as well as indigenous job creation. Secondly, it will investigate the wider experiences of self-employed teleworking in the countryside and, more specifically, the extent to which the experiences of individual teleworkers, and organisations using them, are sustaining or inhibiting rural telework.   Finally, the book attempts to establish the extent to which certain factors, for example organisational change, the aspirations of individual teleworkers, and telework facilitation policy, are underpinning the development of self-employed telework in rural areas.

Since the development of self-employed telework reflects most clearly recent organisational and employment change, and appears to offer greatest potential for development in rural areas (due to contractual and spatial flexibility), the book focuses principally on self-employed home-based telework. As such, a modified version of Huws et al's (1990, p. 10) definition has been used which includes only self-employed, home-based workers:

> Self-employed individuals who work predominantly at home (at least half of their working time), the location of which is independent of the location of the client organisation and can be changed according to the wishes of the individual teleworker. It is work which relies primarily on the processing and creation of information which relies to a large extent on the use of electronic equipment within the home, the results of which are communicated remotely to the client organisation. The remote communications link need not be a direct telecommunications link but could include the use of mail or courier services.

The book is divided into ten chapters which fall within three parts. Part One comprises the first three chapters which set out the context of the study and the research methodology. Chapter Two provides a broader context to the telework debate through an in-depth synthesis of the existing European and North American telework literature. It begins with a consideration of the wider literature concerning emergent shifts towards information-based work and flexible working patterns, of which, self-employed telework, is a component. It then discusses the issues concerning the development of such working practices within rural areas generally. The chapter moves on to consider recent debates and research on teleworking, in both rural and general terms. It is demonstrated that research into telework has tended to be largely aspatial, ignoring particular geographical aspects of the development of these new working practices. The chapter concludes by conceptualising the development of rural telework within three key processes; supply-side, demand-side, and facilitative processes.

The seven subsequent chapters are concerned with extensive research conducted in Wales and the South East of England. Chapter Three is concerned with describing the research methodology used in the research project. It describes the starting point of the research – a postal survey of telecottages – which provided a context for the study. It then goes on to outline the selection of the two contrasting rural areas in which the in-depth phase of the research was to be focused. The next section is concerned with how interviews with teleworkers, facilitators and organisations were undertaken. Finally, the chapter presents some background information on the two chosen case study areas.

The six chapters concerned with the results of the research are divided into two broad parts: Part Two (Chapters Four, Five and Six) is concerned with three individual surveys exploring the facilitative and demand-side influences on telework in rural areas. Chapter Four, based on a postal survey of 120 telecottages across the UK and Ireland, examines the role of telecottages in facilitating and supporting telework through the provision of ICT, training, marketing and work to teleworkers. Chapter Five investigates in more detail the facilitation of telework within two study areas in rural Wales and the South East of England, through a series of in-depth interviews with key agency respondents including local authorities and development agencies. It explores the role, experiences and perceptions of rural-based agencies in the facilitation of telework (primarily through the development of, and support provided for, telecottages), within the two study areas. Chapter Six considers the demand for telework from organisations. On the basis of in-depth interviews with public and private organisations involved in sub-contracting work to teleworkers within the two case study areas, it investigates the background to, experiences of, and motivations behind the use of teleworkers generally, as well as in rural areas.

Part Three (Chapters Seven, Eight and Nine) shifts the emphasis to individual teleworkers involved in the supply of telework. All three chapters are based upon 52 in-depth interviews with teleworkers in the case study areas of rural Wales and the South East of England. Chapter Seven begins by examining the motivations and factors behind the decision to telework in the countryside. Attention is then shifted in Chapter Eight to the characteristics and dynamics of the teleworking situation and the extent to which telework is locationally independent of client organisations. Finally, Chapter Nine considers the wider experiences of teleworking in the countryside, the advantages and disadvantages of telework, and the degree to which present experiences may influence the decision to remain in, or to leave, self-employed telework.

Chapter Ten brings together the key findings to form a comprehensive summary and conclusion.

2 The Information Economy and the Emergence of Rural Telework

2.1 Introduction

It has been acknowledged that during the 1980s and 1990s changes within the rural economy have mirrored those of Britain as a whole, particularly in relation to the service sector, of which self-employed telework is a component (Townsend, 1991, Cloke et al, 1994, 1997). Thus, it is important to locate the development of telework in rural areas within a broader context of economic restructuring and changing patterns of work at the national and international level.

Whilst, as will be demonstrated, research into rural teleworking has been minimal, a wider sociological and geographical literature exists on the development of information-based self-employment and small firms in non-metropolitan spaces. A consideration of this wider literature not only provides a broader academic context to the development of rural teleworking but also raises important issues which have been absent from research into telework more specifically.

The chapter begins by exploring emergent shifts towards information-based employment and the development of self-employment and small businesses. It then examines the debates surrounding the development of these new business activities in rural and non-metropolitan spaces. The remaining sections focus more specifically on research which has been undertaken into self-employed teleworking in a general and rural context.

2.2 The emergence of the information economy and flexible working patterns

The economies of advanced capitalist societies are clearly undergoing fundamental changes and this is linked to the shifting importance of non-material commodity production processes, exemplified most clearly in the increasing proportion of the workforce who are no longer involved in making tangibles (Burrows and Curran, 1989, p. 533).

It has been widely acknowledged that society is moving into an information age where the acquisition and manipulation of information and knowledge is becoming the predominant economic paradigm (Bell, 1974, Toffler, 1980). Indeed, while the service sector has superseded manufacturing as the dominant sector of employment, the most spectacular service growth in the last 20 years has been in the so called producer, or business services (Daniels, 1986, Britton, 1990). Business services support production rather than consumption and include predominantly information-based activities. They are commercially based functions serving 'intermediate' demand from public and private organisations across all industrial sectors, as opposed to final consumer demand. Information-based business services have been defined as 'any exchange between two agents in which the abilities (the 'expertise') of one are acquired and influence the behaviour of the other' (Wood, 1991, p. 162).

Wood (1991) also suggested that information-based business services characteristically deal in white collar expertise and include management consultancy, market research, advertising, public relations, personal recruitment and training, provision of consultancy advice on marketing, computer and data analysis, communications, financial management, commercial law and property management. Although he placed emphasis on the 'expertise' involved in the service, other commentators have included forms of work which involve lower levels of expertise, but which are still involved in the processing and creation of information. These include freelance journalism, typing services, translation, document copying, tabulating and duplicating, graphic design, product design, advertising and marketing (O'Farrel et al, 1993b, Keeble et al, 1991a).

There has been a considerable amount of evidence presented which indicates a massive growth of employment within this sector during the 1980s and 1990s. Wood et al (1993) reported that employment in the Standard Industrial Classification 'other business services', which includes most of the work types identified above, grew in the UK by 158%, compared to a growth of 6.8% in all other industries and a decline of 13% in manufacturing between 1981 to 1989. They also indicated, that, although large and small firms were involved in this growth, it was small firms (with less than £500,000 turnover) which accounted for the majority of the growth, many of which comprised sole traders.

In addition to the growth of small information-based firms, there has been a widely documented increase in self-employment and particularly of self-employed individuals with no employees over the 1980s and early 1990s. Using data from the labour force survey, Cambell and Daly (1992) reported that the number of people in Britain who were self-employed as their main job increased by 1.1 million (52%) to a total of 3.3 million between 1981 and 1991. They also indicated that over 66% of the total self-employed population were individuals with no employees, with over 90% of the reported growth of self-employment falling within this group. In 1991 self-employed individuals with no employees accounted for 69% of the total self-employed population, just over 9% of the total economically active population (OPCS, 1991).

It is also apparent that much of the recent growth of self-employment has been within the 'business services' sector. Cambell and Daly (1992) showed that between 1981 and 1991 the levels of self-employment in the 'financial services' and 'other services' sectors grew by 119% and 104% respectively, while self-employment across all sectors only increased by 52%. Data from the OPCS (1981, 1991) has highlighted that much of the growth in these sectors had been amongst the self-employed with no employees, with a growth in the 'banking and finance' and 'other services' sectors of 50% between 1981 and 1991.

A considerable number of these new entrants to small scale self-employment and those setting up single person businesses, particularly those involved in information-based business services, are basing themselves at home due to convenience and cost. Granger et al (1995) for example, undertook research on self-employed workers in the UK book publishing industry and suggested that because many of the occupations involved, (for example desk-copy editors, proof readers, illustrators, indexers), are characterised by low task interdependency and require little expensive equipment (for example, computers), the jobs are very suitable for freelance working at home. Keeble et al (1991a) also argued that the development of new information technologies is facilitating the growth of home-based professional self-employment (i.e. self-employed telework).

While it alone cannot explain the high formation rates, the low capital investment and high labour input required for information-based-businesses generally has facilitated the growth of small scale self-employment within these sectors (Wood et al, 1993). The development of professional accreditation in areas such as management consultancy and market research has also reassured clients about the standards of provision, making the use of independent freelancers by large organisations increasingly acceptable. Finally, it can be argued that the low overheads of small firms enable them to charge lower overheads than larger enterprises, thus making them more competitive.

2.3 The development of information-based enterprises within the rural economy

In terms of the growth of small firms generally in rural areas, there has been a larger increase in the number of small businesses in rural, as compared to urban, areas since the 1980s. This concentration of expertise and specialist businesses in rural areas reflects the quality of life and residential attractiveness of the countryside to professional entrepreneurs who have underpinned the growth in SMEs in such areas (Keeble, 1993). Much of this growth has been attributed to the urban-rural shift in manufacturing employment and the emergence of flexible specialisation - the development of new forms of skilled craft production within innovative regional economies which foster a harmonious equilibrium between competition and co-operation between firms (Gilbert et al, 1992).

However, in terms of the growth of the service sector and more specifically information-based enterprises, of which telework is a component, it is evident that areas which possess an existing concentration of professional staff and large organisations are likely to exhibit higher than average small business formation rates. This is due to the importance of previous employment in large organisations to the successful establishment of small businesses. For instance, several studies have demonstrated that the most important facilitator to small firm establishment has been previous work experience (Cooper, 1981, Jenssen and Kolverid, 1991, Birley and Westhead, 1994). Such attributes have also been important in determining the motivations, characteristics and performance of these small businesses. As such, Keeble et al (1991b) stated that:

> the most important attributes possessed by the entrepreneurs who established these firms are professional expertise and an existing reputation and a network of client contacts. These essential requirements for competitive success explain the marked concentration of founders' immediately previous employment in same sector or client firms (p. 6).

In a further study, Birley and Westhead (1994) found from a postal survey of 744 small business service firms in the UK that a significant proportion of business founders established their venture in the same industry as their last employer. Additional research has found that former companies have actually given support to the establishment of the new business through sub-contracting work to them (Wood et al, 1993). It is therefore clear that large firms are the most important incubators of new entrepreneurs providing training, expertise, reputation and networks of contacts including potential clients for new business.

Consequently, Wood et al (1993), in a survey of small business services firms in the UK, reported that a significant proportion of the growth in small business service firms had been biased towards the South East to the detriment of other regions, due to the concentration of industry and commerce in that area. They claimed that, although some dispersal of expert employment may have taken place into rural areas, the most highly specialised functions such as management consultancy and market research have been concentrated in this region.

However, one of the central arguments of the telework debate has been that developments in ICT have reduced regional influences on the location of small business service firms, as the providers of such services no longer need to be located near the clients buying in their services. For example Wood (1991) stated that:

> communications improvements have made some services increasingly tradable, no longer requiring close co-location with clients. (p. 165) [and]
> ... the falling real costs of communications and computer equipment mean that small business service firms can reach diverse and widely distributed clients (p. 168).

Several studies have supported these statements. In a postal questionnaire survey of 425 business service firms in Scotland and the South East of England, O'Farrel et al (1993b) found that growth in employment in business services between 1985 and 1990 was virtually identical. In a further study, Keeble et al (1991a) reported that a large number of small business service firms, particularly the individual home-based workers, have been established in rural or small town environments. Finally, Wood et al (1993) stated that a significant number of small business services are located in rural or small town environments, facilitated by modern communications allowing accessibility to major economic centres. They also indicated that lifestyle factors may be of importance in leading to a dispersal of such activity, as professionals, who form the basis of business service growth, choose to live in more preferable, largely rural, locations.

Despite the evidence pointing to the existence of business service firms in non-metropolitan and non-traditional workspaces, the degree to which services are being undertaken for remote, urban markets appears constrained by a number of factors. For instance, the requirement for many information-based service providers to interact closely with clients on a face to face basis has meant that close co-location must exist between service providers and consumers, meaning that such businesses would be restricted to serving local or regional markets. Wood (1991), for example, stated that certain services, such as management consultancy, advertising and market research, depend on intimate interaction with the client and this applies even if the resulting information is processed and communicated remotely through telecommunications. He subsequently argued that there exists a remaining need for certain levels of face to face contact between service providers and clients, which telecommunications cannot replace. In addition, Thrift (1994) suggested that intensive use of telecommunications and increasing levels of information communicated internationally may actually lead to an increased, rather than a decreased, use of face to face contact in order to decipher and make sense of such information.

The extent to which ICT can be used to market services to companies and ultimately secure contracts remotely has also been questioned. In a questionnaire of 58 manufacturing firms in mid Wales, Hitchens et al (1994) found that in terms of the use of business service firms, face to face contact was important for initially locating and recruiting firms to undertake the work, even if the enterprise was not proximate.

The perception of remote businesses by organisations can also be viewed as a militating factor against their use. For example, O'Farrel et al (1995), in interviews with 81 business service firms in Ireland and Scotland, found that the firms considered their ability to compete in distant markets limited because they considered that organisations would perceive them as 'far away and culturally distinct' and not a 'serious competitor in business services' (p. 127). This issue was compounded by the fact that service products are intangible and firms were unable to demonstrate the quality of their service to potential clients. Securing contracts in these instances thus became heavily reliant on reputation.

However, several studies have demonstrated that the constraints listed above are not as dominant as has been suggested, and as such, implying that business success is not dependent on location and proximity to markets. Beyers and Alvine (1985) reported that business services were increasingly being traded and mediated to non-local regions, while, based on research into information-based business services in Scotland and Nova Scotia, O'Farrel (1993) discovered that there was a considerable reliance on distant markets by these firms. In a further study based in Denmark, Illeris (1994) explored the need for close co-location between small business service firms and companies. He found that for routine 'back office' services such as word processing, data processing and bookkeeping, once tasks had been defined, all information was transmitted by telecommunications, and there was little or no need for personal meetings between producers and consumers. As such, proximity played a limited role in the location of service firms. For specialised services such as technological innovation, software development and market research, many face to face meetings were required and, because of this, the costs of meetings were minimised if the producer was located near the consumer. However, he suggested that because such services were unique and expensive, even the considerable costs incurred in overcoming distance did not play any significant part in the decision to utilise or provide a particular service. Clearly, quality was a more decisive factor than location.

In conclusion, while there is evidence indicating the existence of small information-based businesses in rural areas, the extent to which work is being undertaken for remote, principally urban markets is still relatively unknown. Through the in-migration of workers with established clients, remote rural areas can be recipients of business activities based upon remote, urban markets. However, how these working arrangements are sustained by maintaining present clients and through acquiring new clients has not been considered by any research. Furthermore, it is also unclear how, and if, these telework opportunities are available to those indigenous groups marginalised from mainstream employment and without skills developed within largely urban based markets.

Clearly, this broader academic literature raises a set of issues which are relevant to the telework debate. The remaining sections of this chapter will now consider research which has focused more specifically on teleworking within the rural and general arena.

2.4 Recent debates concerning rural teleworking

Since the early 1970s a whole host of academic, policy and popular publications have focused on telework predominantly as a 'techno-centred' panacea for many socio-economic problems facing contemporary society. For example, telework has been associated with increasing labour market flexibility; facilitating employment creation, particularly in economically disadvantaged regions; reducing levels of commuting, pollution and general transport problems; and enabling those who wish, or are restricted, (such as those with childcare responsibilities) to work from home and enter the formal labour market.

The possibility of a redistribution of information-based work away from traditional industrial centres has also generated considerable interest in the potential geographical implications of telework and, in particular, how rural areas may be recipients of these new working practices. Certainly, inherent in many popular notions of telework have been the idea that it is currently, or could be, a predominantly rural phenomenon. Huws et al (1990) stated that:

> One of the most arresting images in the public imagination of our times is that of a lone figure at a computer terminal, perhaps in an isolated rural setting, linked, as it were umbilically, to employers and the rest of the world only by an electronic cable (p. 1).

Indeed, early telework commentators linked its development to the de-centralisation of production and employment through changing patterns in the organisation of production. Toffler (1980) for instance, suggested that the 'Third Wave' of economic change which superseded the 'First' and 'Second Waves' (the agricultural and industrial revolutions respectively) would facilitate a de-urbanisation of employment and a shift back to a pre-industrial landscape based on hi-tech homeworking, from what he termed the 'electronic cottage' (p. 204). For example, he stated that:

> Apart from encouraging small work units, apart from permitting a decentralisation and de-urbanisation of production, apart from altering the actual character of work, the new production system could shift literally millions of jobs out of factories into which the Second Wave [industrialisation] swept them and right back where they came from originally: the home (p. 204).

However, despite these popular notions of telework, the image of an isolated worker communicating remotely with other people has led to concerns about the ways in which telework could lead to lower levels of face to face contact, psychological and social isolation and a breakdown of human relations. However, Toffler (1980) has argued that such concerns are largely unfounded:

> The popular fear that computers and telecommunications will deprive us of face-to-face contact and make human relations more vicarious is naive and simplistic. In fact the reverse might very well be the case. While some office or factory relationships might be attenuated, bonds in the home and the community could well be strengthened by these new technologies. Computers and communications can help us create community (p. 382).

Certainly, visions of an isolated rural homeworker 'plugged in' to international networks of information, and yet being integrated into people and place based community networks, have received considerable attention from the popular media, policy makers and particular fractions of capital. It has been proposed, for instance, that such possibilities have proved to be a powerful fantasy for many workers, particularly those wishing to escape the rigours of urban life and to work in a remote rural idyll through the use of information and communication technologies (Bibby, 1995, Gillespie et al, 1995). Indeed, shifts in the economy are, in many ways, linked to processes of population change and socio-cultural composition within many areas of rural Britain. Many commentators have pointed to the existence of a rural idyll - notions of close knit community, healthy problem-free lifestyles in the countryside - as a powerful motivation behind in-movement to certain rural areas (Newby, 1985, Little, 1987). It has been suggested that such rural in-migration can be further facilitated by the opportunities generated through telework. Cloke et al (1994) for example, stated that:

> on a small scale the growth of homeworking and telecottages [in rural areas] is likely to be lifestyle led (p. 59).

Indeed, representations of telework, particularly within the popular media and certain policy publications, have often been rooted in notions of a shift in lifestyle:

> Mrs Ingram's office is now a room of her cottage at Deeping St James, eight miles outside Peterborough. The view is of her garden down to the river. She feels fitter, no longer having a back problem aggravated by packed trains, and has time for swimming, aerobics and a more active part in her community (Bannister, 1993, p. 4).

> The growth of teleworking is already underway as computer programmers, freelance journalists, lawyers, architects, designers, insurance actuaries and others hang up their pin-stripes and swap the carbon monoxide of rush hour commuting for the fresh flow of country air through the window of the spare bedroom that has been converted into a home-based office (Rural Development Commission, 1990, p. 6).

Such characterisations have also been accompanied by pictorial representations of telework, focusing on the juxtaposition of a lifestyle based on working in an office in a city to one based on living and working at home in the countryside (see, for example, the front cover of Bibby, 1998). Indeed, certain fractions of capital have been exploiting the link between teleworking and a 'rural lifestyle'. British Telecom (BT) produced a series of newspaper advertisements and marketing material advocating telework. These advertisements were illustrated by photographs and impressions of an isolated cottage, with ivy around the porch and roses in the garden. Bibby (1995) reported that one of the advertisements read:

> Instead of you always going to the office, the office can come to you. All you need is a phone socket, a desk that overlooks the garden and the right equipment (p. 1).

Of course, the 'right equipment' needed to be purchased from BT, which is what the advertisements were marketing. Another illustration is that of Acorn Televillages, a commercial property development company, which has developed a site in Crickhowell, a picturesque village in the Brecon Beacons National Park in Powys, into a Televillage. Upper House Farm, a series of 17th Century listed buildings, has been converted into a hi-tech village with fibre optic network links in each house so that residents have the opportunity to telework. Underlying these developments is the marketing of rural areas as desirable places to live, combining healthy lifestyles with the attraction of close knit, place based communities where people live and work. This is illustrated in the Acorn Televillage Brochure, entitled 'Acorn Televillages, Communities that work':

> People no longer need to commute to the cities. Many jobs can now travel to the workers using today's technologies - revitalising traditional rural communities ... And there is a determination of more and more people to achieve a better quality of life, avoiding the stress and pollution of commuting, and playing more active roles day to day in their communities (Acorn Televillages, undated, pp. 2-3).

In addition to these idealised notions of telework, the possibility of a redistribution of workspaces away from urban centres has generated considerable interest, particularly from those agencies responsible for the well-being of rural areas. This interest has focused on the potential of telework to regenerate rural areas, both socially and economically, through the creation of service-based jobs 'plugged in' to remote, often urban markets. As such, teleworking has been viewed as being able to stem the out-flow of skilled labour in search of better employment, facilitate the diversification of the economy and enable those marginalised by location to enter mainstream employment. For example, the European Union ORA (Opportunities for Rural Areas) programme, (part of DG VI) reported in 1993 that:

> as agricultural employment has declined, the economic and social fabric of society in some areas risks to disintegrate ... The combination of new

information and communication technologies ... offer an opportunity to break the spiral by allowing a much greater diversity of employment to be based in rural areas ... (p. i).

Such interest has been mirrored at national level by many rural development bodies in the UK, including Action for Communities in Rural Areas (ACRE), The Highlands and Islands Enterprise (HIE), Development Board for Rural Wales (DBRW), Training and Enterprise Councils (TECs), Rural Development Commission (RDC), and other community groups keen to investigate and develop teleworking opportunities in rural areas. For example, telework has been seen as a new way in which to attract successful individuals and small businesses to rural areas as a form of inward investment. This is demonstrated by the following excerpt from a Highlands and Islands Enterprise marketing brochure:

> The combination of opportunities for teleworking - with workers employed in homes and offices 'remote' from central offices - and an attractive lifestyle make the Highlands and Islands a great place to spread your wings (Highlands and Islands Enterprise, undated, p. 1).

Notwithstanding the general desire of certain agencies to increase levels of telework in rural areas and the portrayal of an idealised image of teleworking in the countryside, an increasing trend towards this type of rural teleworking might result in a set of add on problems for rural areas. For instance, an increased in-migration of those fractions of the service classes keyed into electronic modes of working could lead to a more intense gentrification of certain areas:

> Some Utopian views foresee the abolition of the spatial disadvantages of rural dwelling, as telematics allows rural dwellers full participation in the economic, social and cultural opportunities of urban society ... The reality is more likely to involve a hollowing out of rural society ... where only those with skills relevant to the (urban centred) information economy can survive, leading essentially suburban lifestyles in a rural landscape (Kelleher, 1995, p. 31).

Furthermore, Stanworth and Stanworth (1991) have suggested that such a trend may increase the fear amongst rural pressure groups, such as the Council for the Protection of Rural England (CPRE), that telework may bring in relatively well-off incomers from urban centres, pushing up rural property prices and forcing indigenous people to towns and cities in search of cheaper accommodation. Teleworking has also been linked with the integration of a dispersed, fragmented and marginal labour force into mainstream labour markets. Indeed certain forms of telework have been associated with low skilled data processing and clerical work (Huws, 1984a), which raises issues of exploitation of rural labour markets as corporations seek to reduce office and labour costs. Webster and Robins (1979) have pointed to additional problems associated with these new working practices generally. They have indicated that the re-invention of domestic production in terms of home-based teleworking forms part of a strategy of organisations to undermine the working class enabling corporations to side step worker organisation and subsequently enforce lower wages and a reduction in job security. Such critiques have also viewed telework as reinforcing domestic production by women and perhaps, paradoxically, maintaining rather than liberating, their position in the home. These views have been re-iterated by certain trade unions, fearing the creation of electronic sweatshops and the extension of home-based working (Walsh, 1992).

2.5 Previous research into rural telework

Whilst the last three decades have witnessed a considerable interest in rural teleworking, much of the in-depth and more rigorous research into telework has steered clear of the rural arena. Although certain studies have explored geographical aspects of telework and in a few cases rural telework, much of the research has been based upon secondary data analysis and anecdotal examples, whereas the more detailed research has often drawn conclusions which have not been substantiated by the findings.

For example, Korte et al (1994), on the basis of interviews with telework employers across Europe, suggested that telework is more likely to take place in urban and suburban areas as opposed to the countryside, due to the concentration of industry and commerce in such areas. In addition, Huws (1993) also on the basis of research into teleworking organisations reported that:

> These results give no support to any argument that teleworking is most likely to be found in rural areas. On the contrary, it seems more likely to be found where population density and land values are high. These areas of relatively high telework prevalence tend to be ones where traffic is congested and commuting times are long (p. 6).

However, both authors made these assumptions on the basis of research into the location of teleworking organisations and not on the location of teleworking individuals. Both interpretations imply that teleworking individuals will be spatially proximate to teleworking organisations, which takes no account of the possibility, at least, that such workers could be located in a rural area.

Other studies have, on the other hand, reported that rural areas have been recipients of these new work practices. Huws et al (1996), on the basis of secondary data, used particular telework 'indicators' such as levels of homeworking, self-employment, workers involved in non-manual occupations, to highlight potential telework activity in rural areas of England. They suggested that self-employed or freelance telework, involving skilled professionals undertaking occupations such as computer programming, writing, and consultancy, has the potential to be based anywhere, but is concentrated in 'middle England'. Full-time home-based employed telework, on the other hand (where the person is employed by one sole organisation), is most likely to be based in peripheral rural areas.

Through observations of a small number of teleworking enterprises in the Highlands and Islands of Scotland, Gillespie and Richardson (1994) reported that rural areas have been recipients of successful teleworking enterprises, although they found that the initiators of such enterprises tended to be incomers to the area. Based upon similar research, Hendersen (1994) also observed that the Highlands and Islands of Scotland had attracted a number of homeworking individuals because of the better quality of life, and the possibility of still being able to sell their services to remote markets. Such individuals included software writers, translators, designers, financial analysts and consultants, bringing high value operations to remote rural areas.

Finally, a project commissioned by the European Union to explore the psychological aspects of telework in rural areas, undertook a questionnaire survey of 192 teleworkers across the UK, Germany, Holland, Ireland and 'other countries' (PATRA, undated). The questionnaire considered the perceptions of both rural and urban teleworkers and found that rural telework was considered less expensive and more attractive by respondents, although infrastructural barriers (maintaining equipment and supplies and quality of telecommunication links) were more important for rural than urban teleworking.

Given the lack of in-depth and rigorous research on telework in rural Britain, there is clearly a need to look further afield and consider academic studies of telework beyond the rural arena. This enables other issues, such as the characteristics, experiences and the factors behind telework more generally, to be examined. It is to this literature that the chapter will now turn.

2.6 The nature of the tele 'work'

Gillespie et al (1995) argued that the European Union's statement that telework can create new jobs is based upon a misunderstanding of the nature of telework. They stated that:

> A telework job is not a new type of job, but rather an existing type of job - whether an architect, a designer, a secretary, a computer programmer, whatever - which is carried out in a new way (p. 148).

Certainly, it is generally accepted that telework principally involves information or knowledge based occupations where tasks can be processed and transmitted via ICT to clients, from remote workspaces such as the home. Subsequently, certain authors have produced comprehensive lists of the types of jobs that are 'teleworkable', including both routine functions, such as data and word processing and more specialist and professional services such as consultancy. Stanworth and Stanworth (1991) identified five types of teleworkable jobs based on the fact that they all involve the handling, processing or retrieval of information, rather than the production of a tangible product: These were:

1) **Professionals and management specialists** - including architects, accountants, managers, market researchers, public relations and human resources personnel, financial analysts and brokers;

2) **Professional support workers** - for example bookkeepers, translators, proof-readers, indexers, researchers;

3) **Itinerant field workers** - including company representatives, surveyors, inspectors, property negotiators, auditors, journalists, insurance brokers;

4) **Information technology specialists** - for instance systems analysts, software programmers and engineers;

5) **Clerical support workers** - such as data entry and word processor operators, directory enquiry staff and tele-sales staff.

Similar lists of teleworkable occupations have been suggested by Di Martini and Wirth (1990). Not surprisingly, all of these types of work mirror closely those identified within the broader academic literature as being part of the information services sector. Research into telework generally has also tended to reaffirm that information-based occupations are most suitable for telework. A number of studies have also demonstrated that telework is most prevalent amongst professional occupations as opposed to more routine occupations such as word and data processing. For example, in a study of 84 home-based teleworkers in the UK, Fothergill (1993) found that occupations were broadly grouped as accountancy, counselling, translating, consultancy/business, computing and writing/publishing/editing. Similarly Huws (1984b) discovered that over 90% of the 78 home-based teleworkers she studied in the UK were professionals as opposed to clerical staff.

2.7 The extent of telework

There are no official statistics which can directly indicate the growth or prevalence of self-employed, as well as other forms, of telework in most European and North American countries, let alone in rural areas of Britain. One of the reasons for this is the problem of definition - as telework encompasses a range of working practices and is a way of working rather than an occupation. However, the lack of official statistics has led many commentators to produce guesstimates. In terms of the wilder estimates, Nilles (1985) suggested that there would be 10 million people using ICT to work at home in the USA by 1990. The Henley Centre for Forecasting (1989) offered more realistic figures, reporting that there were about 100,000 employed teleworkers and 500,000 self-employed teleworkers in Britain. Gray et al (1993) provided some statistics detailing specific numbers of different types of teleworkers in the UK and America, based on the integration of a number of different studies. The problem, which they admitted, was that such figures were based on 'guesstimates' from a 'few reliable responses' (p. 273). For the UK they stated that out of a 27.4 million economically active workforce, 2.08% are self-employed teleworkers or employees of small businesses, 0.22% are teleworking employees of large organisations who spend the majority of time at home, 0.51% are teleworking employees who spend a minority of the time at home and 1.82% mobile teleworkers.

One survey has offered more empirically grounded estimates based on a large scale survey of organisations. Huws (1993), in a survey of 1003 organisations across a range of regional, sectoral and size variables, found that only 58 were considered genuine telework employers, which could be generalised to 6% of all organisations in the UK. However, Huws (1993) stated that this figure generated from her research excluded self-employed teleworkers.

2.7.1 The extent of teleworking in rural Britain and Britain as a whole: Evidence from the OPCS

It is possible, however, to extract from official statistics figures relating to the various components of telework - namely information-based employment and homeworking - and where possible to cross tabulate these variables to generate a more reliable figure of the extent of teleworking in rural areas of Britain. While the use of these variables would include a figure for both self-employed and employed teleworkers, the analysis is simply intended to give an idea of the possible extent of all types of home-based telework in rural, as well as other areas of Britain.

Table 2.1 shows those groups of people working at home who would most likely be involved in telework, that is the professional 'service classes' and those involved in non-manual occupations. It also includes all counties and regions of Britain, ranked by the percentage of those in all non-manual occupations (Social Economic Groups (SEG) 1-6)) working at home. These groups include employers and managers, professional workers, intermediate and junior non-manual workers. Even with the exclusion of all manual occupations and those involved in hospitality and agricultural sectors, which may give rise to a bias in rural areas, it can be seen that by identifying Townsend's (1991) 22 rural counties, there is a clear over-representation of these non-manual homeworkers in rural areas of Britain.

2.8 Factors behind the growth of telework

While most commentators agree about the considerable growth in the last decade of information-based self-employment, and therefore self-employed telework as a component of this growth, there exists some divergence regarding the mechanisms underpinning such changes. For example, a humanistic approach would link the development of self-employed telework to the internal motivations of human agency in terms of individual teleworkers. As such, psychological motivations, such as individual enterprise and non-work aspirations, could be solely attributed to the development of telework. On the other hand, a political economy approach would place the emphasis on the economic and social structures determining the adoption of telework by inidviduals and the conditions under which they work. For example, the growth of telework has been linked to organisational restructuring, externalisation and increases in sub-contracting which have facilitated organisation flexibility to cope with increased competition and fluctuating markets.

Table 2.1   Proportion of non-manual workers (SEG 1-6) working at home in Britain, by county and region, 1991 (Based on 1991 Census)

	County/Region	Non-manual workers working at home
1	**Orkney**	**4.90**
2	**Western Isles**	**4.34**
3	**Highland**	**4.20**
4	**Cornwall and Is. Of Scilly**	**3.85**
5	**Shetland**	**3.78**
6	**Powys**	**3.69**
7	**Gwynedd**	**3.66**
8	**North Yorkshire**	**3.62**
9	Dorset	3.56
10	**Somerset**	**3.51**
11	Surrey	3.51
12	Isle of Wight	3.45
13	West Sussex	3.42
14	**Dyfed**	**3.35**
15	Inner London	3.25
16	**Borders**	**3.23**
17	East Sussex	3.20
18	Oxfordshire	3.16
19	**Dumfries and Galloway**	**3.14**
20	**Devon**	**3.11**
21	Buckinghamshire	3.07
22	Hereford and Worcester	3.07
23	Gloucestershire	2.96
24	**Lincolnshire**	**2.95**
25	**Norfolk**	**2.94**
26	Suffolk	2.85
27	Cambridgeshire	2.82
28	Hertfordshire	2.81
29	**Shropshire**	**2.78**

30	Kent	2.77
31	Berkshire	2.68
32	Hampshire	2.66
33	Warwickshire	2.61
34	Avon	2.59
35	**Cumbria**	**2.49**
36	**Wiltshire**	**2.48**
37	**Tayside**	**2.42**
38	**Grampian**	**2.41**
39	Derbyshire	2.37
40	Cheshire	2.30
41	Clwyd	2.28
42	Outer London	2.25
43	Gwent	2.24
44	**Northumberland**	**2.22**
45	Essex	2.21
46	Bedfordshire	2.18
47	Lancashire	2.16
48	Nottinghamshire	2.16
49	Northamptonshire	2.11
50	Durham	2.10
51	South Glamorgan	2.08
52	South Yorkshire	2.06
53	**Central**	**2.02**
54	Leicestershire	2.01
55	Greater Manchester	1.97
56	West Yorkshire	1.93
57	Fife	1.89
58	Humberside	1.85
59	Staffordshire	1.77
60	Lothian	1.76
61	Cleveland	1.66
62	West Midlands	1.65
63	Merseyside	1.61
64	West Glamorgan	1.61
65	Mid Glamorgan	1.58
66	Strathclyde	1.41
67	Tyne and Wear	1.29
	BRITAIN	*2.66*

Bold = Townsend's (1991) 22 rural counties and regions of Britain

From such perspectives, the process of restructuring can be perceived to be a symptom of the crisis of Fordism leading to the emergence of a post-Fordist mode of production and flexible working patterns, involuntarily imposed upon workers through unemployment and redundancy.

However, while humanistic interpretations of economic change offer a crude agent-centred model negating the reality of structural formations to problems of individual and psychological motivations (for example, individual enterprise), structured centred models tend to negate the reality of human agency, reducing individuals to non decision makers, and in political economy terms, view human action as being determined and constrained by the demands of capital. Indeed, it has been proposed that in interpreting the development of self-employment and therefore self-employed telework, it is worth remembering that people make their own history (agency) but not necessarily under circumstances of their own choosing (structure). Subsequently, it has been argued that analysis of both structure and agency is required if one is to make any real sense out of recent changes in employment patterns (Burrows, 1991a).

Certainly, the exploration of both structure and agency has been common within the study of self-employment and the development of information based service firms. Within these studies, structure has characteristically been linked to demand-side processes in terms of the changing requirements of organisations and their role in determining the sub-contracting environment in which teleworkers operate. Human agency, on the other hand, has been associated with supply-side processes in terms of the individual aspirations and motivations of teleworkers (Wood et al, 1990, Korte et al, 1994). It is therefore argued that, for the purposes of this research, attention should be given to both structural, demand-side and supply-side, agency centred processes of self-employed teleworking.

It is also important to recognise the role of certain agencies who are acting as telework gatekeepers. For example, the development of telecottages and other telework promotion strategies by certain development agencies is clearly an attempt to link the supply of telework, in terms of potential teleworkers, with the demand for telework in terms of organisations wanting to use teleworkers. Such facilitative and regulatory practices clearly need consideration within the research.

On the basis of these arguments, the following sections will discuss the nature of the structural changes leading to a growth in the 'demand' for telework from organisations, the role of human agents in the 'supply' of these new work practices and how certain telework 'facilitators' have played a part in linking the 'demand' for, and 'supply' of, telework.

2.8.1 Telework demand and organisational change

Recent discussion on economic restructuring and employment change in Britain has focused on the crisis of Fordism and emergent shifts towards flexible working practices and increasing flexibility in the capitalist mode of production, for example, Harvey (1989) has stated that from the late 1970s:

> corporations found themselves with a lot of unusable excess capacity ... under conditions of intensifying competition. This forced them into a period of rationalisation, restructuring and intensification of labour control (p. 145).

More specifically, it has been suggested that the organisation of production within advanced capitalism has witnessed a major qualitative shift towards flexible production, founded on a network of sub-contracting relationships in place of large scale mass production systems (Scott, 1988). This makes sense of the relative labour market structure since the mid 1970s, that is the massive increases in self-employment and small businesses, reported earlier. Furthermore, inherent within such developments has been the fact that the service industries generally have superseded manufacturing as the main sector of employment in Britain. The growth of the service sector has been considered to be due to both a relative increase through the externalisation of services from manufacturing enterprises and an absolute increase in the demand for particular services as information processing and the acquisition of knowledge becomes essential for competitive advantage within an increasingly globalised economy (Daniels, 1986, Britton, 1990).

With reference to such developments, Wood (1991) has stated that the growth of small information-based firms reflects a considerable increase in the expenditure of organisations on external consultancy and other information intensive services. Wood subsequently advocated that any understanding of this growth must be seen in the context of the changing requirements of organisations and more specifically the decision to sub-contract tasks as opposed to carrying the skills in-house.

One influential illustration of the changing employment practices within organisations was proposed by Atkinson and Meager (1986) and was termed the 'flexible firm'. It was argued that a 'flexible firm' was one which attempted to secure three types of organisational flexibility: numerical flexibility in the ability to expand and contract the workforce in line with fluctuations of demand; functional flexibility in the ability of key staff to transfer skills in line with market changes; and financial flexibility to facilitate numerical and functional flexibility. The resulting labour market structure was based on a core and peripheral workforce, the core consisting of staff providing key specialist skills in constant demand which were well paid in return for their willingness to change tasks and acquire new skills. Numerical flexibility was obtained by going outside the organisation to secure the services of a peripheral group of sub-contractors and self-employed specialists. This peripheral group has generally been seen to be providing routine functions and peripheral jobs with low job security. However, it has been acknowledged that vital non-routine organisational, technical, marketing and trading services are also provided by this peripheral group, including highly specialist sub-contractors, as they are beyond the expertise or capacity of in-house resources (Wood et al, 1993). Indeed, in support of such theoretical perspectives, Wood et al (1993) stated that:

> In broad theoretical terms, the impressive growth of business services may be credited to falling transaction costs and the evident benefits to many organisations of employing competitive outside suppliers of specialist expertise, rather than increasingly costly in-house sources (p. 679).

Implicit within the flexible firm model has been the vertical disintegration of organisations and associated externalisation, whereby previously internal functions have been substituted with external sub-contractors such as self-employed individuals. This has had the effect of creating new small business opportunities and encouraging individuals into self-employment because of the changing contractual demands of organisations. Externalisation has been viewed as a mechanism for reducing the permanent workforce and associated overheads such as office rents and sick and holiday pay and replacing them with the transaction costs of sub-contracting (Atkinson, 1984, Atkinson and Meager, 1986, Marshall, 1988). This model therefore places the growth of information based self-employment (for example, telework) within the context of labour process changes and structurally imposed constraints on the opportunities for, and outcomes of, the workforce.

Externalisation has also been linked to the growth in the number of quasi-employees - those registered as self-employed to enable the company to avoid National Insurance and tax contributions. Academics have therefore argued that to equate all self-employed individuals without employees with 'one person businesses' would be a mistake (Burrows and Curran, 1989, Dale, 1986, 1990). Differentiation of quasi-employees from truly self-employed workers has focused on the relationship between the client and the worker. The client-worker relationship of quasi-employees is considered to be a dependent one, where work is undertaken for one sole client. Those conforming to more rigorous definitions of self-employment, and as such having autonomy and independence in the work process, are seen to work for multiple and changing clients (Dale, 1986, 1991, Burrows and Curran, 1989). Research on home-based telework has shown that teleworkers who mirror closely the characteristics of quasi-employees have been involved in temporary, part-time and often low skilled work at home (Huws 1984a, Allen and Wolkowitz 1990). Truly self-employed teleworkers on the other hand have been involved in more professional occupations (Huws 1984b, Haddon and Silverstone 1993, Fothergill 1993).

The growth of these new sectors has also been attributed to an absolute increase in demand for new services engendered through international recession, rapid technological change, internationalisation of competition, deregulation and privatisation inherent in radical government policies (Bryson et al, 1993). Business services such as market research and consultancy have been seen to be increasingly critical for many aspects of the effectiveness of organisations in the context of changing economic and business environments (Wood et al, 1993). Furthermore, Wood (1991) has suggested that an increase in demand has been created out of considerable technological change where the novelty of such technologies has created a need for specialist advice about their use. He also noted that new technologies have multiplied the amounts of information stored and communicated around the world, and that there is a demand for services to interpret this flood of information. Finally, he explained that, as small business service firms are inherently heavy users of technology, they have been disproportionately affected by such developments and as a result have increased their technological sophistication and in some cases their patterns of specialisation, that is diversifying into, and creating more, technologically orientated business services.

Small firms have also been considered to be the primary source of business services due to the premium placed on the individual professional as the service provider rather than a whole organisation (Keeble et al, 1991a, Wood, 1991, Wood et al, 1993). Certainly, the acquisition of key skills which are not tied to a specific organisation appears to be a major facilitative factor in the establishment of small businesses. Keeble et al (1991a) argued that the nature of the relations supporting service functions favour small firms because of the qualitative and flexible nature of demand. Indeed, the growth of small business service firms has been linked to notions of flexible specialisation and the shift from larger to smaller more flexible units of production (Perry, 1990, O'Farrel et al, 1993a). These shifts involve both technical changes in production and organisation, and changes in labour control towards autonomously self-regulating work groups (Burrows, 1991a). Such systems have also been seen to involve large numbers of technologically advanced firms operating within a network of similar small firms, but linked to larger firms integrated into national and international markets (Piore and Sabel, 1984).

Some of the telework research has pointed to organisational restructuring and associated externalisation and redundancy as a major factor in its development. For example, the most frequently cited examples of telework schemes operated within organisations, F International and Rank Xerox, have both been based on the use of self-employed teleworkers Rank Xerox for example, in an attempt to reduce overhead costs at its central London office in the recession of the early 1980s, encouraged certain employees to set up their own businesses and then continue to work for the company on a sub-contract basis, using ICT to communicate the work. The result was considerable savings on overheads of approximately £17,000 per head (Kinsman, 1986).

2.8.2 Individual workers and the supply of telework

Routes into self-employment, and as such self-employed telework, have been based upon two opposing logics of entry; 'unemployment push'; and 'self-employment pull'; and also 'combinations of opportunities and constraints motivating individuals to become their own boss' (Granger et al, 1995, p. 501). The 'unemployment push' hypothesis relates closely to structural constraints, as discussed in the previous section, characterised by the employment policies of large firms and the condition of the labour market during periods of recession and increased competition. More specifically, it is associated with the effects of redundancy and forced unemployment (for instance, through formal externalisation) by encouraging individuals into self-employed telework.

The 'self-employment pull' hypothesis, on the other hand, links the development of self-employment more specifically to the choices of individual agents and the attractions of being one's own boss (Bogenhold and Staber, 1991, 1993). In this sense, teleworkers are themselves involved in initiating and transforming the structures of demand through exerting pressure on organisations to adopt more flexible working arrangements in order to accommodate their own aspirations.

Research into individual teleworkers largely discounts such external factors (for example formal externalisation and redundancy) as a major influence on the growth of self-employed telework. Studies have tended to demonstrate that motivations behind telework in Britain have related closely to the attractions of self-employment per se rather than a reluctant shift into self-employment (Huws et al, 1990, Fothergill, 1993, Haddon and Silverstone, 1993, Gillespie and Richardson, 1994).

These findings also appear to mirror research into self-employment more generally. For example, from 472 interviews with new self-employed entrants in Britain, Hakim (1989) highlighted that, although most people mentioned more than one reason for becoming self-employed, the desire 'to be one's own boss' was the dominant motivation given by the respondents. Although she did report that only around one quarter of respondents could be classified as involuntary or at least reluctant entrants to self-employment, amongst this group 'push' factors were often complemented by more positive reasons for establishing the business. Moreover, she stated that redundancy and unemployment often provided a catalyst for individuals to undertake what they had wanted to do for some time. Other studies of self-employed individuals have found that, while many people had been unemployed prior to establishing the business, unemployment was not necessarily the key motivating factor. Rather the attractions of self-employment were perceived as the real cause (Carter and Cannon, 1988, Storey et al, 1988, Granger et al, 1995).

Homeworking

Research into self-employment has often pointed to the decision to work at home as a consequence of small scale self-employment rather than a key factor in the decision to become self-employed. For instance, the low capital and spatial requirements of information-based businesses have meant that the home has been a more suitable, cost-effective work space than a rented office (Hakim, 1988, Keeble et al, 1991a, Fothergill, 1993). However, a significant volume of the telework literature has focused on homeworking as a key motivation behind individual decisions to telework, particularly in terms of accommodating certain non-work requirements. For example, self-employed telework has been viewed as providing a way of integrating work and certain childcare and other caring. Indeed, 25% of teleworkers studied by Fothergill (1993) gave childcare responsibilities as the main or only reason for working at home. In other studies, Huws et al (1990) found that 36.1% of 119 home-based teleworkers in the UK and Germany had given up their previous situation to have a baby, while Christensen (1989) in her survey of 215 female teleworkers in America reported that many women work at home as a way of balancing childcare responsibilities. Christensen (1989) also reported that women tended not to work and care for their children simultaneously but often work when the children are asleep or when their partners could care for them. Other telework research has re-iterated these findings (Huws, 1984a, Olson, 1988).

Remote working

Previous sections have highlighted the opportunity to work at a distance from urban centres as one of the main attractions of telework. Olson (1988), for example, suggested that telework precludes the need to commute, enabling individuals to engage in improved lifestyles through an increased involvement in recreational activities, such as 'ski[ing] in the middle of the week when there are no crowds' (p. 82)! It has also been mentioned that telework may facilitate a rural lifestyle through the ability to live and work in the countryside. Indeed, as mentioned earlier, Gillespie and Richardson (1994) found that teleworkers studied in the Highlands and Islands of Scotland tended to be incomers to the area, attracted by the perceived advantages in lifestyle.

Other issues

It was noted earlier that factors motivating individuals to become self-employed are not necessarily the same ones which retain the worker in that situation (Bogenhold and Staber, 1993, Granger et al, 1995). For example, telework has been linked to increased levels of social isolation and worker productivity and also feelings of insecurity due to the short term nature of contract work. These in turn have been linked to the exploitation of marginal labour markets by organisations. As such, the extent to which teleworkers have been able to exercise the flexibility and autonomy often associated with self-employed telework can be seen to be constrained by the demands of capital. However, certain commentators have suggested that those workers most likely to have such experiences are those who have been forced into telework (Huws et al, 1990). Certainly, it appears that the identification of the processes behind the adoption of telework by individuals also provides a clear indication as to the extent to which telework more generally is constrained and determined by individual motivations and aspirations or by the demands of organisations.

Previous sections have highlighted that entry, by workers, into information-based self-employment, and as such telework, may be greatly facilitated by the networks of client contacts, reputation and expertise developed within former (often urban-based) employment. It can therefore be suggested that the establishment of a remote (and potentially rural-based) working situation is greatly facilitated by contacts within, and knowledge of predominantly urban-based markets. Clearly, in this sense, such workers already have means to establish links with clients directly through the self-marketing of their skills.

However, for certain groups, such as indigenous rural dwellers, the opportunities for the development of such experience may be limited. For instance, Gillespie and Richardson (1994) found that many teleworkers studied in the Highlands and Islands were incomers to the area who had established reputations, expertise and networks of client contacts in largely urban centres prior to moving to the countryside. They also claimed that these attributes were unlikely to have been established in remote regions and concluded that to establish key 'urban' contacts remotely would be difficult.

The development of telecottages and other telework facilitation strategies in rural areas by certain agencies have been specifically developed to address this problem. This has been through facilitating the link between the supply of teleworkers, in terms of those individuals wanting to telework in a rural area, with the demand for telework, in relation to those organisations outsourcing work to such workers. The role of such facilitative factors will now be considered.

2.8.3 Facilitative factors

It was indicated in earlier sections that certain agencies responsible for the social and economic regeneration of rural areas have been keen to encourage and facilitate the development of teleworking in rural areas. For example, Johnston (1990) stated:

> Applications of information technologies offer the possibility of reducing the remoteness of rural areas from other regions or parts of the Community. As information and communication technologies essentially provide a means of communicating and processing information, the economic constraints imposed by geographical location which have characterised rural areas will become less significant ... Applications of information and communication technologies can facilitate economic growth in rural areas, by allowing the movement of firms to people, rather than vice versa (p. 21).

Indeed, due to the beneficial qualities attributed to telework, it has entered the public policy agenda. A recent report of the European Union's High

Level Group on the Information Society (1994), entitled 'Europe and the Global Information Society: Recommendations to the European Council' (better known as the Bangerman Report), provides a good illustration of the enthusiastic adoption of telework and its priority in terms of public action. The report proposed:

> the promotion of telework in homes and satellite offices so that commuters no longer need to travel long distances to work ... Companies (both large, SMEs, and public administrations) will benefit from productivity gains, increased flexibility and cost savings. For the general public, pollution levels, traffic congestion and energy consumption will be reduced. For employees more flexible working arrangements will be particularly beneficial for all those tied to the home, and for people in remote locations ... (p. 4).

Perhaps the most significant manifestation of the desire to facilitate telework in rural areas from European, national and locally based agencies, has been through the development of telecottages, which have been loosely characterised as:

> workcentres with hi-tech equipment where people can be trained, bring along their own work, or do work supplied by the centre (Coles, 1992, p. 53).

and which provide access to

> open learning courses and self-tuition, access to information technology and telecommunications services ... and generally ... to information exchange and work (Denbigh, 1992, p. 5).

Indeed, telecottages have been viewed by a range of social and economic development agencies in rural areas as the primary tool for the facilitation of telework in the countryside. By way of illustration, the report 'Current Experiences and Perspectives for Teleworking', DG XIII (European Union 1992) made three recommendations for action in terms of telework, each focusing on the provision of a telematics centre or telecottage. In addition Moseley (1990), the then Director of ACRE commenting on a report on telecottages, suggested that:

> This report describes a new weapon in the armoury of rural development, for while the telecottage may not be a panacea for all ills, it can certainly offer a solution to many of these problems. We are now in the information age where, as far as desk bound work is concerned, distances are

irrelevant, and telecommunications can provide a commuting medium ... Already telecottages are providing training for rural people, ... services and equipment for use by one person businesses and are now beginning to provide paid work (p. 3).

Certainly, it appears that many telecottages have been established and funded by such agencies in order to facilitate telework in rural areas (Watkins, 1989, Denbigh, 1990, 1991). According to the literature, the aim of the telecottage concept has been to provide low cost access to, and training in, ICT (for example computers, modems and faxes), aimed at helping those individuals wishing to telework but without the necessary skills or equipment to do so. They also aim to support established teleworkers seeking a workspace outside of the home or specialist advice and equipment. However, perhaps their most important role has been to create telework directly - establishing links between individuals wanting to telework, and organisations wishing to use teleworkers. This has been through establishing a 'telebureau' within the telecottage - a form of on-line employment bureau - marketing the skills of teleworkers to remote, urban based companies and then importing work into the area, via ICT and outsourcing the work on a contract basis to local, home or telecottage based teleworkers (Finch, 1991, Moindrot, 1991, Batt, 1992). In this capacity telecottages provide a corporate front for a pool of teleworkers, which can approach, and be approached by, companies wishing to outsource work to teleworkers. As such, they can be viewed as simply a sub-contracting enterprise attempting to appropriate and facilitate the flexible labour use strategies of companies by encouraging them to outsource tasks to teleworkers via the telecottage.

At the commencement of the research for this book in 1994, there had been no research conducted which had explored the nature and extent of telecottages in Britain. However, the development of telecottages has been documented to a limited extent in the national media, a series of telecottage seminars and in a national teleworker magazine. This publicity has been produced principally by the Telecottage Association, a charitable organisation established by ACRE and the RDC in 1989 to promote and support teleworking and telecottages in the UK. In addition, since a telecottage survey was undertaken as part of this book, two studies have since been published (and as such should be considered). One was carried out by Murray (1995) on behalf of the Telecottages Association and the other by CURDS (Centre for Urban and Regional Development Studies 1995).

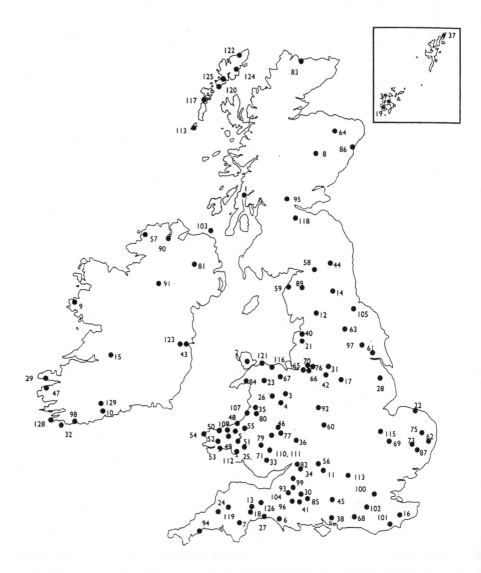

Figure 2.1   Location of British and Irish Telecottages, 1995

Source: The Telecottage Association, 1995

Dobbs (1990) reported that there were no telecottages in the UK until the 1980s, although he suggested that there was great enthusiasm for the idea and proposals for telecottages were springing up all over the UK. In response to such enthusiasm, ACRE and the RDC established the Telecottages Association in 1989, and in 1992 a similar organisation, Telecottages Wales, was set up in Wales. The establishment of these associations has acted as a catalyst for the growth of telecottages, and in 1999 there were 152 operating in the UK (Telecottages Association, 1999).

Whilst it is acknowledged that telecottages are not specifically a rural phenomenon, their growth appears to have been particularly concentrated in the more peripheral areas of the UK (see Figure 2.1). This observation was substantiated by both the CURDS (1995) and Murray (1995) telecottage surveys which indicated that over half of the telecottages surveyed were located in remote rural areas or in small towns and villages. Indeed, it would appear that the term tele'cottage' itself has been constructed from a certain 'rural' discourse.

It is also evident from the literature that a large number of telecottages have been established by community groups and public agencies, with funding provided by local authorities, Training and Enterprise Councils, Enterprise Agencies and the European Regional Development Fund (ERDF) and European Social Fund (ESF) (Watkins, 1990, Consortium of Rural Training and Enterprise Councils, 1991, Denbigh, 1991, 1992). In fact both CURDS (1995) and Murray (1995) reported that, in terms of ownership and funding, the majority of telecottages were publicly run and managed, with only a small number being set up and run privately by individuals. As CURDS (1995) stated:

> telecottages represent a principal (and often only) information and communications technology policy response of local authorities and other agencies charged with economic development (pp. 61-62).

Clearly, it is evident that the desire of certain agencies to encourage the development of telework in rural areas has been a major factor in the growth of telecottages in such areas.

Telecottages have been particularly linked to the growth in telework due to their role as telebureaus - creating telework opportunities for local people. For example, Antur Tanat Cain Telecottage in Wales secured a contract from ICL, the computer company, to undertake data processing. The work was outsourced to around 40 home-based self-employed teleworkers who had been previously trained in ICT skills at the telecottage. The project was successful and set an example of how a telecottage overcame remoteness by gaining access to markets beyond the local area through the use of telecommunications, creating locally based employment opportunities.

Other examples have been Devon Teleworking which had a contract to edit text for Reuters, and Argyll Community Telematics which was linked to an electronic medical publishing project for Elsevier (Cohn, 1992). It is also evident that certain telecottages and teleworking networks have been involved in establishing skills registers and marketing strategies for local teleworkers (Batt, 1992, EDAW Ltd, 1996).

However, while telecottages have been linked to the growth of telework, through the development of the 'telebureau' concept, both telecottage surveys discovered that the main role of telecottages was perceived by managers to be training, with the provision of access to ICT, business services and workspace hire, rather than the marketing of, and securing work for, teleworkers (CURDS, 1995, Murray, 1995). While both studies found that a number of telecottages had created employment, neither offered evidence to suggest that this was in fact telework, that is work sourced and communicated remotely from organisations via the telecottage to local teleworkers. Indeed, CURDS (1995) stated that, overall, telecottages were only making a minimal contribution to employment creation through telework.

This view was reiterated by a report commissioned by Telecottages Wales which found that there was little reliance on telecottages by typically successful teleworkers (EDAW Ltd, 1996). These teleworkers were considered to be:

> those which had worked in large urban centres, developed valuable skills, and had established a network of contacts from which to generate work (p. 4).

In addition, it was reported that:

> there was limited evidence of those trained solely in IT skills/teleworking at telecottages progressing directly into employment using these skills (p. 4).

2.9 The experience of self-employed telework

While the previous sections have discussed the various factors leading individuals into self-employed telework, it has been claimed that factors motivating individuals to become self-employed are not necessarily the same ones which retain the worker in that situation (Bogenhold and Staber, 1993, Granger et al, 1995). This argument can be similarly translated to self-employed telework. Thus, while it appears that dominant motives behind self-employed teleworking have related to the positive attractions of autonomy and temporal, spatial and residential flexibility, it can be argued that the extent to which people stay in that situation will depend on the experience of self-employed, home-based, remote working. Moreover, it has been recognised that transitions into, and potentially out of, self-employment are embedded in a 'dynamic context of social and economic circumstances' (Bogenhold and Staber, 1993, p 469). Therefore, as personal or economic circumstances change, the attractions and advantages of self-employment over conventional employment may also change.

Within the telework literature, a set of distinct advantages and disadvantages have been attributed to telework (Di Martini and Wirth, 1990, Huws et al, 1990, Stanworth and Stanworth 1991). It was argued earlier that previous telework research has given insignificant consideration or recognition of contractual status when interpreting the experience of telework. As a result the experience of homeworking has often been confused with the experience of self-employment. For example, Fothergill (1993) stated that 'the advantages and disadvantages of working at home may sometimes be indistinguishable from those of self-employment generally.' (pp. 11-12). Key aspects of both the self-employment and the homeworking experience therefore need consideration.

2.9.1 The experience of self-employment

Leighton (1982) has suggested that self-employment generally has been linked with particular individualistic attitudes termed the 'philosophy of self-employment', emphasising flexibility, autonomy, choice and freedom in the work process. More specifically, self-employed teleworking has been associated with certain levels of flexibility - temporal flexibility in terms of organising home and work life and flexibility in terms of the work types undertaken and organisations served (Robertson, 1985, Stanworth and Stanworth, 1991). These types of flexibility are heavily advocated in Charles Handy's 'portfolio lifestyle':

> Portfolio people put their different bits of work into different folders, rather as architects do, or journalists, and sell their services through examples of their products. At times, one client, one product will fill up the portfolio ... But more and more, as other responsibilities, including parenting, need time and attention, and as our powers and interests expand, our portfolios will diversify (Handy, 1985, pp. 27-28).

These observations have been supported by research into predominantly self-employed teleworkers. For example, Fothergill (1993) found that flexibility, control, independence and the general advantages of 'being one's own boss' were given by respondents as the primary advantages of telework. However, Hakim (1988), on the basis of in-depth interviews with self-employed individuals in the UK, found that within certain forms of self-employment there exists an illusion of autonomy and control which is grasped tightly as it helps to compensate for the realities of working long hours, being even more tied to their work and being dependent on their bank managers, as opposed to employers. Similarly, an in-depth study of predominantly self-employed teleworkers by Haddon and Silverstone (1993) revealed that in reality teleworkers had little control over levels of work. They found that the short-term nature of contracts meant work was unpredictable and workers found it difficult to say no to work when it was offered, leading to considerable amounts of over working. Fothergill (1993) also demonstrated that, while the majority of respondents felt they had autonomy and freedom in the work process, about a quarter expressed feelings of insecurity in terms of work and cash flow. Regardless of this evidence, both of the latter two studies reported that in reality feelings of insecurity were unwarranted, because in the majority of cases problems were clearly associated with too much work, rather than too little work.

Quasi-employees, registered as self-employed to enable the company to avoid National Insurance and tax contributions, on the other hand, are not deemed to experience the advantages of autonomy and independence associated with conventional self-employment. They are considered to provide dependent, sub-contracting roles, providing a peripheral existence and peripheral jobs (Dale, 1986, 1991, Burrows and Curran, 1989).

2.9.2 The experience of homeworking

As for homeworking, telework facilitates many opportunities, particularly for those restricted to, or who wish to, work at home. It has already been indicated that one of the most cited advantages of telework has been how it can allow the integration of work and childcare responsibilities. However, certain studies have highlighted the difficulties experienced in attempting to combine childcare and work. Consequently it has been reported that many teleworkers have found it necessary to employ some sort of childminder to enable them to work more effectively at home (Gordon and Kelly, 1986, Haddon and Silverstone, 1993).

The narrowing of the gap between professional and home life through teleworking can be viewed as creating a set of potential conflicts within the home. In research into female homeworkers, Allen and Wolkowitz (1987) found that working in the domestic sphere incorporated other work obligations enforced by the demands of other family members in terms of domestic responsibilities. Haddon and Silverstone (1993) highlighted the difficulties experienced by teleworkers in terms of separating out work and home space. For instance, they found that the integration of home and workspace made it difficult for teleworkers to mentally switch off from work and these problems were compounded by the actual or perceived threat of continual interruptions from the fax or phone.

Many researchers have also pointed to the potential problems of both professional and social isolation in the homeworking situation. Indeed, Huws et al (1990) suggested that isolation and the lack of interaction with colleagues found in more conventional working environments was one of the major disadvantages of, and inhibitors to, the widespread adoption of telework. Telecottages have been considered to play a vital role in this respect by providing communal workspaces for teleworkers attempting to escape the problems of working at home, but to retain the advantages of working in the local area (Watkins, 1990, Denbigh, 1991, 1992). A number of studies into telework have demonstrated that social isolation has been a considerable problem for home-based teleworkers (Diebold Group, 1981, Huws, 1984a, Huws et al, 1990, Fothergill, 1993). Moreover, it has been suggested that women are more likely to experience isolation because of the tendency to be involved in more routine functions (Kawakami, 1983). However, Huws et al (1990), in relation to all forms of home-based telework, argued that those who experience social isolation the most are those workers that have been forced into telework and as a result are most conscious of the disadvantages of their situation.

Certain writers have also pointed to the potential problems of professional isolation in terms of the lack of intellectual stimulation through interaction with colleagues. For example, Stanworth and Stanworth (1991) suggested that professional isolation is particularly evident for those (such as self-employed teleworkers) who are recruited from external labour markets and as such are not involved directly with organisations. Both Haddon and Silverstone (1993) and Fothergill (1993) found in their survey of teleworkers in Britain that the lack of external support and stimulation from colleagues was a significant problem for them.

Another argument given within the literature has been that a decrease in interaction with work colleagues through homeworking may increase levels of interaction at the local level within the community, and subsequently develop new community feelings (Toffler, 1980, Blanc,

1988). Although Fothergill (1993) reported that a number of teleworkers felt more integrated in the local community because of their homeworking situation, Stanworth and Stanworth (1991) stated that there appears little definite evidence supporting the opinion that telework may increase levels of community involvement.

2.9.3 Future aims and aspirations of self-employed teleworkers

While studies of self-employed teleworking have tended to report relatively high levels of job satisfaction amongst workers (Stanworth and Stanworth, 1991, Haddon and Silverstone, 1993, Fothergill, 1993, Granger et al, 1995), few have examined the future plans of the individuals, particularly in terms of expansion of the teleworking business. However, research into self-employment and particularly individual home-based self-employment has investigated this aspect. Hakim (1989), in in-depth interviews with 33 self-employed individuals in Britain, noted that often feelings of autonomy and independence, which were seen as one of the attractions of self-employment, were similarly expressed in respect to not wanting to expand the business. Hakim also found that motivations to remain small were accompanied by psychological and ethical aspirations. Nonetheless, she suggested that such aspirations were likely to decrease after the initial conception of the business, when workers become aware of the growth potential of their business, although there was no empirical basis for this assumption. Curran et al (1986) also suggested that the assumption that small businesses will inevitably grow into large businesses is unfounded and argued that many of the factors which lead them to set up on their own are indeed the same factors that motivate them to keep the business small.

2.10 Summary

This chapter has demonstrated that there has been little research into rural teleworking, particularly from the perspective of individuals undertaking these new work practices in the countryside. Furthermore, it is evident that research into telework more generally has tended to be largely aspatial, failing to consider the possible location of telework and ignoring other spatial aspects of the nature and development of telework. While an examination of the more general telework literature and the wider academic literature on changing work patterns has highlighted certain issues related to the factors behind, and the characteristics and experiences of, self-employed telework, there remains little knowledge concerning these aspects within a rural context. As such, it is these three key themes on which the research will focus.

Earlier sections proposed that the development of telework in rural areas can be broadly conceptualised by three key processes - demand-side structural processes; supply-side agency centred processes; and public agency led facilitative processes. These processes, along with the actors representing these three elements (organisations, teleworkers and public agencies), form the foci of the research project. Figure 2.2 is a diagrammatical representation of the three key components in the form of a conceptual framework for the research. The diagram highlights the various arenas of interaction between, and influences of, the three processes of self-employed telework. For example, the establishment of the remote working situation can be stimulated by individuals marketing themselves to, and interacting directly with, companies. They can also be developed indirectly, through the telecottage, which approaches companies on behalf of teleworkers and provides individuals with the technology and skills in order to telework. The individual aspirations of those individuals involved in the supply of telework, in terms of the decision to telework and the ability to control the conditions under which they operate, are also clearly evident. These motivations are determined by individual aspirations but they are also influenced and constrained by external factors. Such external influences include organisational change and the demand for more flexible working practices from companies. As such, the supply of telework can be seen to be dependent upon combinations of opportunities, individual aspirations and structural constraints which influence the motivations behind, and characteristics and experiences of, telework. The diagram also shows the demand-side processes of telework and how the organisational structures facilitating telework are influenced by structural shifts towards more flexible modes of production and also by the demand by individual workers for more flexible working practices.

The main themes to be addressed within this book, initially presented in Chapter One, outlined how the research is concerned with an exploration of the characteristics and experiences of, as well as the factors behind, teleworking in the countryside. The conceptualisation developed in this chapter permits an examination of these key aspects through a consideration of the motivations of individual telework agents as well as the wider structural processes and the more locally based facilitative factors which also appear to have influenced and shaped its development. The following empirical chapters address these issues through an investigation of the various actors representing the three components of the

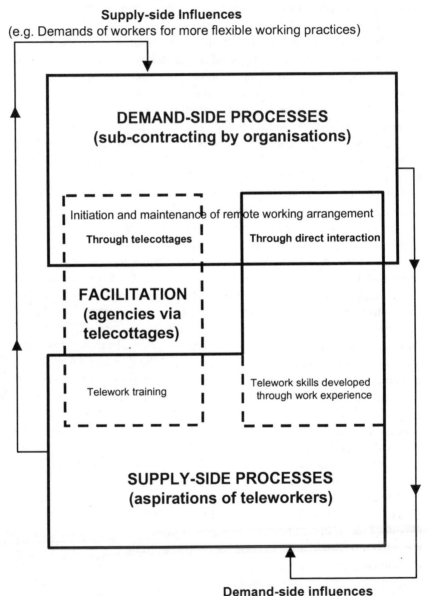

Figure 2.2   A model of the interactions between, and influences of, the processes of self-employed teleworking

conceptual framework. For example, the research explores the motivations, characteristics and experiences of individual teleworkers involved in the 'supply' of these new work practices in two rural study areas; the characteristics, experiences and motivations of organisations involved in the 'demand' for self-employed teleworkers in such areas; and the 'facilitation' of telework through an examination of the roles, perceptions and experiences of agencies involved in attempting to stimulate the development of telework in the study areas as well as through a consideration of the role of telecottages in facilitating telework in rural areas more generally. Before proceeding into the results of the research, however, the next chapter explains the research methodology and the nature of the case study areas chosen for the in-depth phase of the research.

3 Research Methodology

3.1 Introduction

The previous chapters have provided the context for the research project and outlined the conceptual framework and a set of key issues to explore. It was suggested that in order to elucidate the experiences and characteristics of telework, as well as the factors underpinning its development in rural areas, a consideration of three key components is required: the facilitation of telework, through the development of telecottages and other telework facilitation strategies by particular development agencies; the individual teleworkers involved in the supply of telework; and the demand for telework in terms of organisations using teleworkers. This chapter discusses the research methods used to explore these various elements and describes the two rural case study areas in which the in-depth phase of the research was undertaken.

3.2 The Telecottage Survey

It was decided that the most appropriate starting point for the research would be an exploration of the nature and role of telecottages in facilitating telework. Such a study would provide a broader context for the subsequent in-depth study of teleworking in the countryside. Of particular interest in this phase of the research was the reasons why telecottages were being set up; how they were attempting to facilitate telework; and how successful they were in creating new teleworking opportunities in the local area.

It was intended that the comprehensive list of telecottages given in the Teleworker - the Magazine of the Telecottages Association, would form the sample for the study. Despite earlier indications that telecottages appear to be a predominantly rural phenomenon, it was not possible from this list to differentiate 'rural' from 'urban' telecottages. An additional aim of the survey was therefore to establish the degree to which telecottages are a rural phenomenon. All 129 British and Irish telecottages listed in the January 1995 issue of the Teleworker were therefore included in the survey.

It was decided that a postal questionnaire would be the most appropriate form of data collection considering the number and location of

48

telecottages, and the relatively uncomplicated nature of the information required. The questionnaire utilised a mixture of pre-coded closed questions and open ended questions. The questionnaire was divided into four sections reflecting the aims of the survey. The first concentrated on the background of the telecottage - primary functions; number of employees; ownership; income and reasons behind its establishment. The second considered the role of the telecottage in facilitating telework through the outsourcing of work; the types of tasks involved; numbers of individuals involved; client base; and how the work is distributed. The third section focused on the nature of other teleworkers known of by the telecottage; the role of the telecottage in maintaining a skills register of teleworkers; and the marketing of teleworkers. This section also explored the characteristics of the work and workers and the use of the telecottage by these individuals. The final section considered issues relating to the location of the centre; problems associated with securing work; and future plans for the telecottage.

A pilot survey of 20 telecottages was undertaken in early February 1995, with ten of these being returned within a two week period. As a result, small alterations to two questions were undertaken to avoid any possible mis-interpretation. Following these amendments, the revised questionnaire was distributed to the remaining 109 telecottages throughout Britain and Ireland in February. Follow up reminder telephone calls were made to telecottages which had failed to respond after a month of sending out the questionnaire. The survey resulted in 52 (42.3%) successful completions being returned by the end of April 1995.

3.3 Selection of the case study areas for the in-depth phase

It was intended that the in-depth research of teleworkers, client organisations and facilitative agencies would be undertaken within two contrasting rural areas, reflecting the different geographies of rural Britain - one which was close to concentrations of industry and commerce, and another remote from such activity. This was in order to explore whether geography, in particular proximity to concentrations of commercial and industrial activity, influenced the development of telework.

After much consideration, the counties of Dyfed and Powys were chosen as the remote rural case study area as they exhibited a very high concentration of telecottages, and as such provided an ideal area in which to explore the effectiveness of agencies (through telecottages) in influencing the development of telework. The counties of Surrey, East and

West Sussex, and Kent were chosen as the more pressured rural area. Although they exhibited a lower concentration of telecottages, Chapter Two highlighted how areas in the South East of England generally have particularly high concentrations of potential telework activity, through proximity to commercial activity and high levels of professional non-manual staff. Figure 3.1 shows the location of the two case study areas, which hereafter will be referred to as the Wales and the South East case study areas.

As a final note, it is important to acknowledge that there has been considerable debate over what constitutes 'rural' (see Halfacree, 1995). The word 'rural' is used within this study to denote non-metropolitan spaces, distant from major urban centres and traditional centres of work. Although clearly the South East case study area includes large towns, for example Brighton, such areas can be considered non-metropolitan and non-traditional centres of employment located in predominantly rural districts. Indeed, towns such as Brighton and others on the South Coast represent popular destinations for the retired and those individuals seeking non-metropolitan lifestyles.

3.4 Description of the case study areas

Before proceeding into the specifics of the in-depth research phase, the next section in this chapter provides some background information for the two case study areas.

3.4.1 Employment characteristics

While it was suggested in Chapter Two that available statistics do not provide actual numbers of teleworkers, the following section uses particular variables (for instance, levels of homeworking; employment in the business services sector and numbers of self-employed workers with no employees), to provide an indication of potential telework activity within the case study areas. These figures have been sourced from the 1991 Census of Population (OPCS, 1991), which although now quite dated, are the only source of such indicators at the appropriate spatial scale.

The service sector dominates employment in both study areas, with the highest levels of employment in the 'other services sector', accounting for over a quarter of the total workforce in these areas (Table 3.1).

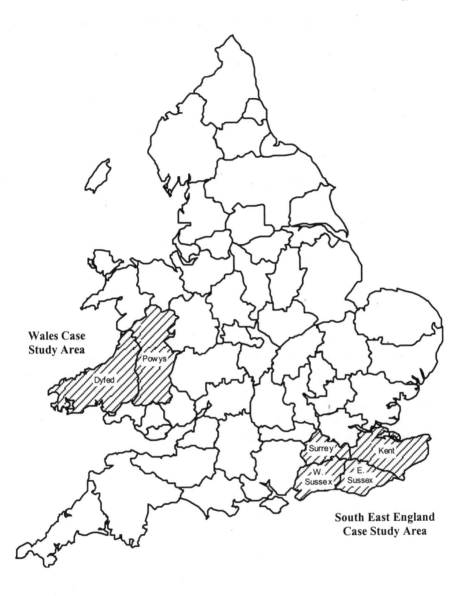

Figure 3.1   Location of the two case study areas

Table 3.1   Sectoral structure of employment in the case study areas, 1991 (%)

Employment sector	South East	Wales
Agriculture	1.87	10.55
Forestry and Fishing	0.10	0.60
Energy and Water	1.49	2.77
Mining	2.13	1.87
Manufacturing	6.88	5.12
Other Manufacturing	6.10	6.71
Construction	8.01	8.56
Distribution and catering	20.71	20.84
Transport	8.15	4.35
Banking and finance	15.96	5.93
Other services	27.79	31.10
Not stated	0.79	1.60

Source: 1991 Census

Employment in the 'banking and finance' sector in the South East area is approximately three times that recorded in the Wales study area. The occupational structure of each area is broadly similar, although the Wales study area exhibits slightly higher levels of employment within the lower skilled occupations such as plant and machine operatives and craft and related occupations (Table 3.2). The South East study area exhibits a higher concentration of employment within the clerical sector and slightly higher levels in the professional classifications. This evidence demonstrates a higher concentration of occupations suitable for telework within the South East study area.

Table 3.3 shows the growth in self-employment between 1981 and 1991 within the two study areas (note that the self-employment statistics given by the OPCS do not include those directors of their own companies, but who are considered to conform to theoretical definitions of self-employment). While growth in both areas was high, rates in the South East study area were nearly double that of the Wales study area. Moreover, a significant proportion of the growth in the South East area was amongst self-employed individuals with no employees (that is those most likely to operate their business at home), whereas the highest growth in the Wales study area was amongst self-employed persons with employees.

Table 3.2   Occupational structure of all employment in the case study areas by Standard Occupational Classification, 1991 (%)

Occupational type	South East	Wales
Managers and administrators	18.83	20.55
Professional	9.27	7.74
Associated professional	9.58	6.83
Clerical and secretarial	17.11	11.31
Craft and related	12.79	14.61
Personal and protective	9.14	10.00
Sales	7.21	6.35
Plant and machine operatives	7.54	9.61
Other	7.67	11.12
Not stated	0.86	1.79

Source: 1991 Census

Table 3.3   Percentage change in the levels of self-employment (with and without employees) within the case study areas, 1981-1991

Study area	% change in total self-employment	% change in self-employment without employees	% change in self-employment with employees
South East	40.76	57.29	8.87
Wales	22.65	21.94	24.26

Source: 1991 Census

Despite the much higher self-employment rates in the South East compared to the Wales study area, overall, the proportion of workers who are self-employed is significantly higher in the Wales study area than in the South East, with almost a quarter of the workforce self-employed in the former area (Table 3.4). For both areas, self-employment, with no employees forms by far the greatest component of total self-employment, with just over two thirds of those in self-employment in both areas working alone.

Table 3.4   Percentage of persons in self-employment (with and without employees) as a proportion of total employment within the case study areas, 1991

Study area	% total self-employed	% self-employed without employees	% self-employed with employees
South East	14.34	10.12	4.22
Wales	24.70	17.00	7.70

Source: 1991 Census

Both areas exhibit high levels of self-employment within the 'banking and finance' and 'other services' sectors, with around a third of the total self-employed workforce in the Wales study area located within these sectors compared to just under a quarter in the South East study area (Table 3.5). The only major difference between the two areas is that Wales has a higher proportion of self-employed workers in the 'banking and finance' sector than the South East study area.

Table 3.5   Proportion of self-employed workers in the case study areas involved in the 'banking and finance' and 'other services' sectors, 1991

Study area	Banking & Finance	Other services
South East	14.63	7.78
Wales	26.48	6.60

Source: 1991 Census

It was demonstrated in Chapter Two that it is possible to derive potential levels of telework (both employed and self-employed) by looking at those groups of people working at home who would most likely be involved in telework - for example 'professional ' service classes and those involved in non-manual occupations. Table 3.6 shows the growth and extent of homeworking amongst non-manual workers (socio-economic groups (SEG) 1-6) in the two study areas.

Table 3.6   Growth of non-manual workers (SEG 1-6) working at home 1981-1991 and proportion of non-manual workers working at home, 1991, within the case study areas

Study area	% change in SEG 1-6 working at home 1981-91	SEG 1-6 working at home 1991 as % of economically active
South East	48.68	3.16
Wales	38.48	3.44

Source: 1991 Census

Both areas have witnessed a substantial growth of homeworking between 1981-1991, although in the South East study area, growth was nearly 20% greater than within the Wales study area. If one tentatively translates all of this evidence into potential and actual telework activity, it can be suggested that telework is a small but increasing component of the workforce within both study areas. Although the growth of self-employment and homeworking has been greater within the South East area, present levels show that a greater proportion of workers in the Wales study area demonstrate the likely characteristics of actual and potential teleworkers. However, the actual number of workers with these characteristics may be greater in the South East considering the larger populations in this area.

3.4.2 Population change

One aspect of consideration within the research is the degree to which telework is facilitating an increasing in-movement of population into rural areas. A consideration of population change within the two study areas thus provides a context for the investigation in later chapters of telework and rural in-migration.

Champion (1994) noted that the greatest increases in population have occurred in the most remote rural areas of the UK. Table 3.7 shows that the Wales study area has exhibited over twice as much in movement of population over this period compared to the South East area.

Table 3.7   Population change in the case study areas, 1971-1991

Study area	% Population Change
South East	5.11
Wales	11.12

Source: 1991 Census

Since the 1960s many commentators have recognised that population change in rural areas has been accompanied by significant social restructuring with certain localities attracting different types of in-movers. Cloke (1985), for example, has stated that there are several localised variables which act as the predominant elements and which, along with wider structural factors, underlie population change in particular localities. These local factors are land market, physical environment, settlement quality, quality housing market, employment market, social and community factors and accessibility.

Within rural Wales generally, Day (1989) noted that there were three types of in-migrants - the retired, key workers (those who came in to take up employment opportunities) and ex-urban drop outs - spreading into remote areas in search of alternative non-urban lifestyles. Indeed, certain studies of population change in remoter rural areas generally, have shown that the search for a different lifestyle seems to represent a factor in the decisions of households to relocate to these areas (Jones et al, 1985).

Population growth in the South East area, although much less in absolute terms than for the Wales area, can be seen to represent increasing sub-urbanisation from London. Indeed, part of the shift in population in the South East has been attributed to the residential preferences of professional service classes working within London (Wood, 1991), and the search for cultural capital through the acquisition of country houses and estates (Thrift and Leyshon, 1992).

3.5 Selecting a research methodology for the case study areas

The main objective of the research project was to gain an in-depth understanding of the perceptions, characteristics, experiences and motivations of three sets of respondents, namely teleworkers, organisations and agencies, without assuming any prior knowledge of all of the issues. For this reason a quantitative approach was not appropriate. A flexible methodology, such as semi-structured interviews, avoids any pre-categorisation and pre-conceptions inherent in quantitative type surveys, as used in previous studies of telework (see, for example, Huws et al, 1990 and PATRA, undated). Quantitative methods separate the informant from the researcher by a formal questionnaire, preventing more complex interpretations and reducing information to a set of pre-selected variables. They also tend to force replies into particular categories which respondents may or may not have thought about. Qualitative methods, on the other hand, allow the researcher to make interpretations of feelings, values, motivations and constraints which contribute to our understanding of peoples' behaviour. They also enable researchers to relate social structures to individual accounts through the interpretation of text, and subsequently allow understanding of how individuals comprehend the structures they find themselves in.

It was also considered very difficult to communicate with a representative sample of teleworkers. As well as not knowing the total population of teleworkers in the UK, let alone in the case study areas, it was anticipated that the number of teleworkers that could be contacted for interview in the time allocated for this phase of the research would not be high. Huws (1984a), for example, used a variety of methods to contact teleworkers in Britain, such as key telework contacts and adverts in magazines and newspapers, and only managed to gain a sample of 78 homeworkers. Fothergill (1993), using similar techniques and snowballing (asking teleworkers to suggest other potential respondents), managed to find only 84 respondents in the South East and North East of England over a period of a year and a half. Thus, given these issues, and given the in-depth nature of the investigation, a qualitative approach was considered the most appropriate methodology for the investigation of telework in the two case study areas.

Samples drawn from a known population are said to be representative of that wider population and generalisations can therefore be made from these findings to such a population. However, considerable debate surrounds the issue of making generalisations from qualitative data to a wider population (Patton, 1980). However, Dey (1994) has suggested that qualitative research provides a more adequate basis for inferring generalisations than for applying them. This is because it relies on a deeper understanding and analysis of a limited number of cases, thus providing a solid basis for inferences. For example:

> Potential for learning is a difficult and sometimes superior criteria to representativness. Often it is better to learn a lot from an atypical case than

a little from a magnificently typical case (Stake, 1994, p. 243).

As a result, it has been advocated that by exploring a small number of situations in-depth, others can be illuminated without necessarily claiming that they are the same or whether the explanations will always apply (Mitchell, 1983). Given these arguments, the findings of this study should be seen to be indicative, rather than representative of the wider picture.

3.5.1 Interview strategy

It has been suggested that the aim of a qualitative interview is to engage in a conversation, but with a purpose, setting the respondents at ease, and thus reducing the distance between the researcher and the respondent (Burgess, 1992). Such methods provide a flexible way of establishing experiences and interpretations by probing deeply, enabling the researcher to modify a line of enquiry, allowing respondents to raise new issues not previously considered by the researcher and secure vivid and accurate accounts based on personal experience (Burgess, 1992). While a number of qualitative interview styles exist, ranging from structured to un-structured methods, a balance between structure (for ease of analysis) and flexibility (to allow for new issues to be considered) was desired for this research. In addition, Eyles and Smith (1988) have suggested that interviews should not be non-directive or unstructured but based around a framework to encourage conversation along particular avenues and to allow similar topics to be covered by all respondents. As it was intended to compare responses between respondents, without constraining them to a rigid framework of questions, a semi-structured interview style was considered most appropriate. This also enabled the quantification of particular responses within the interview so as to enable a profile of respondents to be constructed. Themes were written down beforehand in the form of an interview schedule, with topics to be discussed. This kept the content and direction of the interviews as similar as possible. Open ended questions left the initiative with the respondent, encouraging communication and allowing the discussion of new topics as they arose, adding to the research content.

The interview schedules and topics to be discussed reflected the key aspects of the research. For the teleworkers, the topics were employment and residential history; motivations behind telework; relationships with, and methods and experiences of communicating and acquiring work from, clients; patterns of work flow; experiences of living and working at home in the countryside; and perceptions and use of telecottages. For the client interviews, themes included background and characteristics of the organisations; background to the use of teleworkers (including organisational change); motivations behind the use of teleworkers both generally and in rural areas; and the experiences of using teleworkers. For the facilitator interviews, issues to be discussed included the motivations behind, and experiences of, promoting telework as well as the nature of the strategies employed to facilitate telework in the study areas.

3.6 Locating and interviewing respondents

Teleworkers

It is widely acknowledged that teleworkers form an almost invisible part of the workforce, and any strategy of contacting them for interview has to consider this element. Huws (1984a), quoting Tahar (1980), has noted that:

> Homeworkers are a notoriously difficult group to reach, and one of the most intractable problems for any researcher investigating their situation is identifying and communicating with a ... sample (p. 23).

Over recent years however, teleworkers have become more visible through the development of various collective structures - teleworking magazines and newsletters (for example the Teleworker magazine and Home Run, a magazine for self-employed, home-based professionals); The National Association of Teleworkers; The Telecottage Association; and individual telecottages. It was anticipated that this research project would utilise these collective structures and key contacts within them to locate teleworkers. Given the lack of research generally into telework from the individual perspective, interviews with those workers undertaking these new forms of self-employment were to form the bulk of the research. Subsequently, considering the problems experienced by previous researchers in locating teleworkers (Huws, 1984a, Fothergill, 1993) and the in-depth nature of this part of the investigation, the intention was that 60 teleworkers, 30 from each area, would be approached for an interview.

In locating teleworkers, adverts and requests were made for respondents which fitted a description based on the definition given in Chapter One. In short, teleworkers were selected on the basis that they were self-employed/single person businesses using a computer and some form of remote communication to undertake the majority of their work from home and for client organisations.

Extensive advertising in shops, libraries and public places in towns and villages was undertaken in both of the case study areas. Requests for respondents were also placed on the Powys Telecentre Network Electronic bulletin board, in the Powys Telecentre Newsletter, the Home Run Magazine for professionals who work from home and on notice boards in telecottages in Wales and the South East study areas. These adverts were supplemented by phone calls to the Teleworker Magazine, Home Run Magazine, telecottages and other contacts.

Responses from the adverts were very low with only two respondents contacted in this way. Problems were also experienced in locating teleworkers connected with, or known, by telecottage managers. It was found through initial telephone calls to telecottages in the study areas that many telecottage managers were either reluctant to provide names of teleworkers, due to confidentiality, or were simply not aware of any teleworkers. By far the most successful method was through the telephone requests to key contacts (for example to the editor of the Home Run Magazine, telecottage support groups and other key telework contacts) and also snowballing, whereby teleworkers were asked to indicate other potential respondents.

The process of locating and interviewing teleworkers was very time consuming and this phase of the research lasted from May 1995 to January 1996. A total of 52 successful face to face interviews (23 in Wales and 29 in the South East study areas) were undertaken within this period. Respondents were contacted by telephone and a face to face interview was subsequently arranged. Interviews were recorded using a micro cassette recorder and lasted between three quarters of an hour and two hours.

Clients and facilitators

As the teleworker interviews were to form the bulk of the research, it was intended to aim for a total of 20 interviews equally divided between clients and facilitators. The client organisations to be interviewed were sourced directly from the teleworkers studied - in that they had been indicated in the interview as past or present clients of the workers. A list of organisations was compiled and either the company, department or personnel manager was subsequently contacted for interview. This resulted in 10 successful interviews, with managers of five private and five public organisations, which were located in or very close to the case study areas. Their distribution reflected the fact that regional influences did influence the client sectors served by respondents. For example, all organisations interviewed in Wales were public sector organisations and all private organisations interviewed were located in the South East. Interviews were undertaken over a one month period in July 1996.

Approximately forty agencies (including Training and Enterprise Councils, local authorities, Rural Community Councils and the Telecottage Association) were approached in order to compile a list of key agencies active in facilitating telework in the case study areas. Ten interviews were subsequently undertaken with respondents from these key agencies, over a one month period in June 1996 (six in Wales and four in the South East).

Four of the client interviews and six of the facilitator interviews were undertaken face to face. Due to difficulties arranging interview times and because of time and resource constraints, the remaining 10 interviews were undertaken over the phone, using the same format as the face to face interviews. All interviews were recorded and lasted between twenty minutes and an hour and a half.

3.7 Analysis of the interview data

While it is accepted that language is not a medium which simply reflects reality, but comprises of notions of reality (Gill and Pratt, 1992), the objective of the interviews was not to engage in an analysis of discourse or semiotics, but an interpretation of the motivations, perceptions and experiences of respondents.

In this respect, it has been suggested that the object of analysis is to determine key themes of the research based on factual information, feelings and opinions derived from an examination of narratives collected from individuals via in-depth interviews (Burgess, 1992, Miles and Huberman, 1994). Concepts are then formed and modified in the light of the empirical data and in the context of a broader framework. Patterns within the data can later be identified and compared with different ideas or theories. Regularities in specific settings then become more gradual and general, obtaining validity outside the specific setting (Sarantakos, 1993).

Whilst there exists a certain amount of literature which attempts to describe how to analyse qualitative data, it appears that much of it is concerned with trying to develop a formal method through the definition of the types of categories that one can use to code data. There have been a number of formal methods developed, for example 'grounded theory' (Glaser and Strauss, 1967) and 'analytic comparison' (Neuman, 1991). However, it has been suggested that most qualitative analysis has involved less well defined approaches, with much of it occurring in the researchers head (McHenry, 1995). It was considered that the best way to understand how to undertake the analysis was through exploring the methods and accounts of other researchers (Okely, 1983, Haddon and Silverstone, 1993, McHenry, 1995).

Dey (1993) suggested that the first stage of the analysis should always involve familiarisation with the collected data. For this reason, interviews were transcribed immediately after the meeting, and a thorough reading of the transcripts was undertaken prior to the analysis stage. Coding or indexing has been seen as the next key process for analysing qualitative data, forming the basis for conceptualising the information. According to Ritchie and Spencer (1994) this process is associated with the cutting and pasting of transcripts, whereby chunks of text are cut out and pasted into headings along with similar items. Although such methods have been criticised for taking the quotation out of its natural context, Richards and Richards (1994) argued that 'retaining a sense of context seems to be linked to a researcher's theoretical assumptions and not just something associated with certain data handling devices' (p. 219). Coding allows the identification of key factors, common relationships and enables an interpretation of the data, making sense of what goes on (Wolcott, 1994).

Given these suggestions, every interview was coded for several main themes. For the teleworker interviews the main themes were as follows - background information (employment and residential history and income); motivations behind their decision to telework; patterns of work flow; client relationships; methods of acquiring clients; experiences of working at home in the countryside; perceptions and use of telecottages; and future plans and aspirations. For the client interviews, themes included motivations behind using teleworkers; background to the use of teleworkers; methods of communicating with teleworkers; and methods of recruiting teleworkers. Main themes for the facilitator interviews consisted of their role in facilitating telework; the nature of telework facilitation strategies; and the perceptions and experiences of facilitating telework.

Coding of the themes involved marking relevant sections from the whole transcript in different coloured marker pens. These coded parts were then entered into NU-DIST, a computer package designed to manage and analyse large amounts of qualitative data. The contents of each theme for all interviews were then printed out and summaries made for each theme and each interview. The next stage of the research involved breaking down these main themes into sub-categories. These were derived through re-reading the text, noting patterns and issues and further sorting with reference to similar and unique patterns and characteristics of events, actors and processes. In practice this involved the cutting and pasting of relevant quotations into different sections.

The result of this process was the creation of a set of broad themes, and sub-categories containing quotations relating to each respondent. While the data in this format enabled description and a level of interpretation to be undertaken, more detailed analysis was required. To facilitate further interpretation and analysis Miles and Huberman (1994) have advocated the use of matrices to summarise and also cross tabulate the data. Therefore, within particular categories, quotations were summarised, usually into two or three words, and placed into a matrix containing a list of all the respondents. This created an instant picture of similarities and differences within the data across the whole sample. To illustrate, in exploring the shift into telework, summaries of respondents' employment history, residential history and key push and pull factors into self-employment were placed into a matrix. This allowed the identification of common motivations, and the linking of these to residential and employment histories. Once such links had been established, a logical chain of evidence was used to support patterns in the research and subsequently develop a particular motivational typology.

3.8 Presentation of the data

Much of the analysis was undertaken whilst writing a first draft of the results chapter. This involved description of the various themes and categories including long segments of quotations. Such drafts were very long with the ratio of quotation to text at about fifty - fifty. While it is normal to use quotations to support the analysis, it is difficult to obtain a balance between description and quotation particularly when the quotes appear more 'alive' for the researcher than the reader. It was felt that although quotes should be used to make their own points, a level of interpretation should accompany this text.

Although qualitative material is in the form of words rather than numbers, Miles and Huberman (1994) have suggested that presenting qualitative data with the aid of numbers is a good way of seeing how robust one's insights are. Therefore, in order to identify particular regularities within the results, it was felt that some level of quantification should accompany the description and interpretation. As the number of respondents interviewed was quite small, the use of actual numbers as opposed to percentages was considered a more appropriate form of quantification within the text. In the chapters discussing the 52 teleworker interviews, actual numbers are used within tables and for ease of reading, terms of quantification are used in the text. For example a 'few' = four or less, 'several' = five to fifteen, 'majority' = 39 (three quarters of the respondents) or greater. Actual numbers in addition to proportions are also used in the text. Where appropriate, numbers of respondents are given for each case study area, for example, (13W/17SE) - 13 respondents in Wales and 17 respondents in the South East study area. Within the client and facilitator interviews, shorthand terms are used to indicate the source of the quotation - that is the client or agency respondent interviewed. These terms are specified in the respective chapters. In the chapters dealing with individual teleworkers, the names of respondents have been changed to retain anonymity. This pseudonym is followed by the details of the respondent's business and location e.g. 'Max, Market Research, South East'.

This chapter has given details of the methodologies involved in the collection and analysis of the data as well as providing some background information for the two case study areas. The next six chapters are based on the results of the four individual surveys undertaken. Part Two of the book (comprising Chapters Four, Five and Six) considers the facilitation of, and the demand for, telework in the countryside, while Part Three (Chapters Seven, Eight and Nine) focuses on the supply of telework in the study areas.

PART 2

The Facilitation of, and Demand for, Telework

4 Telecottages and Telework

4.1 Introduction

Chapter Two highlighted how certain rural-based agencies and community groups have been involved in establishing telecottages across rural areas of the UK and Ireland. It will be recalled that telecottages have been defined as local centres providing access to, and training in, information and communication technologies (ICT). Target consumers are those potential teleworkers without the necessary means, skills, or equipment to work from home, as well as those established teleworkers who may require specialist equipment, advice, or training to enable them to telework more effectively. In addition, telecottages have also been viewed as providing a telebureau, or brokering service, involving the marketing of teleworkers' skills to organisations, securing contracts and distributing the work to local teleworkers.

It was argued earlier that there exists a deficiency of research exploring the nature of telecottages and more specifically their links with, and role in, facilitating telework. The present chapter is based on a survey of telecottages in the UK and Ireland. It attempts to redress this deficiency through an exploration of the degree to which they are facilitating the link between the supply of, and demand for, telework, for example between those individuals wishing to telework and organisations wanting to use teleworkers. In short, Chapter Four considers five key aspects of telecottages.

The location of the 129 telecottages targeted in the survey is indicated in Figure 2.1 (Chapter Two). It was anticipated that the manager of the telecottage, to whom it was addressed, would fill in the questionnaire. A total of 52 questionnaires was received, although one response accounted for a network of seven telecottages in Wales (all providing identical services). This response was included as one entry in the results and, taking this into consideration, the response rate was 42.3%. The distribution of telecottages that responded to the survey is displayed in Figure 4.1.

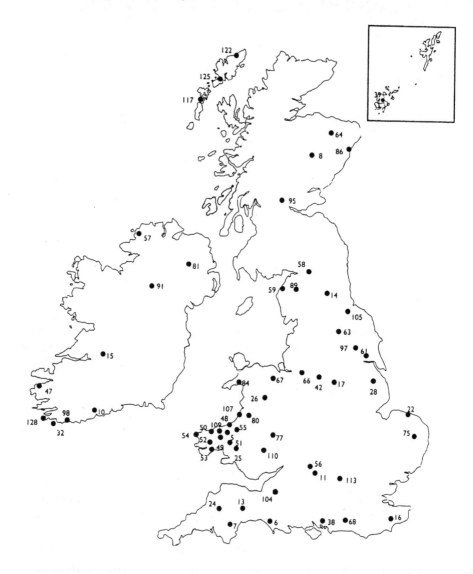

Figure 4.1   Location of Telecottage Respondents

Source: Modified from The Telecottage Association, 1995

4.2 The background of telecottages

Although the oldest telecottage was established in 1979, over 80% had been established in the 1990s when the concept, first introduced from Sweden, became popular in Britain and Ireland (Table 4.1).

Table 4.1 Number of telecottages established by year

Year established	Number of telecottages established
Pre 1980	1
1980-1989	8
1990 +	43
TOTAL	52

The survey requested the selection of one of six categories, ranging from 'remote rural' through to 'urban area' which was most applicable to the location of the telecottage. While it is acknowledged that the selection relied heavily on the perceptions of those telecottage managers answering the question, it was simply intended to give a general picture of location. Only four telecottages were located in large towns and urban areas, whereas over 90% were located in small towns and more remote locations, reaffirming earlier suggestions that telecottages are a predominantly rural phenomenon (Table 4.2).

Table 4.2 Location of telecottages

Location	No. of telecottages
Remote Rural	12
Small Village	15
Large Village	5
Small Town	16
Large Town	2
Urban Area	2
TOTAL	52

The average number of people 'employed' by telecottages (not including teleworkers involved in outsourced work) was 6.3 workers. This number was divided between part-time, full-time, voluntary and other workers. Full-time workers were most common, accounting for an average of 2.2 workers per telecottage. Part-time workers accounted for an average of 1.8, voluntary workers 1.5 and 'other' types of workers 0.8 per telecottage.

4.3 Nature and the main functions of telecottages

In order to establish the nature and main functions of the telecottage, the questionnaire required managers to indicate the nature of ownership, sources of start-up funding and the main functions of the telecottage. In terms of ownership, just under half considered their telecottage to be wholly 'private', a quarter wholly 'public' and the remainder 'community businesses' and 'co-operatives'. Over half, however, indicated that the majority of their start-up income was derived from public sources, such as European Union funding including LEADER and the European Social Fund (ESF), and also from UK based sources such as the Training and Enterprise Councils, the Rural Development Commission, Local Authorities and various regional development agencies, including Highlands and Islands Enterprise and the Welsh Development Agency. Although private funding was less significant in most cases, sources included commercial banks, British Telecom, Apple Computers and the founder's own capital. Further examination of the nature of funding and ownership and the main functions of the telecottage pointed towards the existence of four principal types – 'community businesses'; 'telecottages for the disabled'; 'training centres'; and 'private businesses'.

1. Community businesses (63%) - Whilst this largest group of telecottages exhibited a range of ownership types, including co-operative and community businesses, they could all be considered 'community businesses' - operating as a business in terms of becoming self-sufficient, but receiving significant funding from public sources and operating primarily as a community resource centre. The focus of such centres was low cost access to ICT equipment, workspace, training for local individuals, groups and small businesses and the provision of ICT services such as word processing and Desk Top Publishing (DTP). Although all were involved in ICT training, about a third demonstrated a particular focus on more formal training, each receiving considerable funding from TECs and other sources such as the Further Education Funding Council. Over half of these telecottages were involved in securing contracts from organisations and outsourcing work to local teleworkers. The focus of the community business telecottages was local economic regeneration with a significant community orientation, highlighted by the following quotations:

'[The main aims were] the introduction of IT to the rural community and the exploitation of information technology to enhance the community in a social and commercial way.'

'Our aim is to enable rural communities to exploit their talents through training in information technology and thus enhance employment prospects through the creation and promotion of a pool of marketable skills.'

'[The main aim of the telecottage is] saving the rural community.'

2. Telecottages for the disabled - (7.7%) As with community businesses, these telecottages were publicly funded, focusing on the improvement of employment opportunities through training and access to ICT equipment and services. However, they were primarily geared towards serving disabled people such as those physically disabled or visually impaired. Only one was involved in outsourcing work, typically to disabled workers.

3. Training centres (3.8%) - These two telecottages were wholly publicly funded and operated, and unlike telecottages for the disabled and community businesses, were not aimed towards making profit. They focused solely on the provision of ICT training as opposed to open ICT access, usually in the form of more formal training programmes. Funding for both telecottages came predominantly from TECs.

4. Private businesses (25%) - This group of telecottages had been established and funded by private individuals, and in some cases in addition to the founder's own business such as computer consultancy. Although, as with community businesses, they offered access to training and ICT equipment and services, their objective was profit rather than community development. Greater emphasis was placed on the provision of ICT services such as word processing, desk top publishing (DTP), bookkeeping and software training. Half were involved in outsourcing work to local teleworkers.

4.4 The role of telecottages in facilitating telework through the marketing of, and the securing of contracts for, local teleworkers

The survey revealed that 24 (46%) telecottages had been involved in outsourcing work from external organisations to local teleworkers, working either from the telecottage or from home. Teleworkers consisted of local individuals not employed directly by the telecottage but either self-employed or un-registered workers. Of the telecottages involved, two thirds were community business telecottages and the remainder private business telecottages and telecottages for the disabled.

The total number of individuals involved in the outsourced work was 132 for the 24 telecottages, accounting for an average of 5.5 workers per telecottage. The largest number of workers per telecottage working in this way was 20 and the least, one. Around two thirds of the teleworkers involved were home-based, and of these, around nine out of ten were classified as part-time (Table 4.3). This trend was also apparent for the telecottage-based workers, with a similar proportion working part-time.

Table 4.3   Employment status and workplace of the teleworkers involved in work outsourced by the telecottages

Location of workplace	Full-time	Part-time	TOTAL
Telecottage-based workers	5	43	48
Home-based workers	9	7	84
TOTAL	14	118	132

Eighty three percent of the telecottages which were outsourcing work, distributed some of the work between organisations and between teleworkers electronically. Modems were used by 90%, the fax machine by 65%, with smaller numbers utilising other means of electronic distribution such as X-25 and ISDN. Of those which did not distribute work electronically, the most common form of distribution was sending disks and documents by post or courier.

The dominant types of work outsourced to teleworkers involved routine and non-specialist functions such as word processing and DTP (Table 5.4). These activities were undertaken by around 90% of telecottages which were outsourcing work. Data input and processing were also important components of the work, with just under a third undertaking this type of work. More professional tasks such as software development, programming and graphic design were only undertaken by around 40% of these telecottages. Other, less common types of work undertaken included database management, file transfer, training, translation, journalism and spreadsheet work.

Table 4.4   Types of work outsourced by the telecottages

Type of work	No. of telecottages involved
Word processing	12
Desk Top Publishing	9
Data input/processing	7
Software devp./prog.	5
Graphic design	5
Database management	3
File transfer	2
Translation	2
Training	2
Spreadsheet work	1
Journalism	1
Production of CVs	1
Data analysis/statistics	1

Of the telecottages outsourcing work, three quarters were involved solely with companies in the local area and only a quarter had contracts with large public and private organisations based in other parts of Britain and overseas. Although most used telecommunications technology to distribute the work between organisations and teleworkers, the securing of contracts from organisations involved mainly less technologically-orientated methods, such as word of mouth, contacts in the business, recommendation and to a lesser extent advertising in the local and national press. Only one telecottage manager indicated using e-mail and the Internet for successfully securing work.

Just under half of the telecottage managers reported that they had experienced problems in securing work from organisations, and of these, most were located in small towns or more remote areas. Indeed, many of the rural telecottage managers attributed the lack of work secured from organisations to their geographical peripherality, the lack of demand for their services locally, the perceived remoteness of telecottages by large organisations and the lack of telecommunications infrastructure:

> 'Regional businesses are often in urban areas, and they cannot envisage hi-tech work being done in the countryside - they think the countryside is for farmers and holidays.'

> 'There is little commercial and industrial activity in the area.'

> 'It is an island community and we do not yet have adequate electronic communications facilities on the remote islands.'

> 'ISDN is the limiting factor in rural areas as telecom companies are reluctant to install it on rural exchanges, and if you are more than 2.4 miles from your exchange then it requires an expensive mixer to boost the signal.'

However, one telecottage manager highlighted a key issue relating to a reliance on word of mouth networks for securing work, implying that acquiring contracts from remote organisations was dependent less upon the use of ICT or other forms of remote communications and more on direct, often face to face, interaction with potential clients:

> 'with teleworking, location isn't important, with marketing it is'.

4.5 The use of the ICT, training and marketing services of telecottages by independent teleworkers

In addition to the role of telecottages in outsourcing work to teleworkers, the questionnaire also requested information regarding links with independent teleworkers - those not currently involved in any work outsourced by the telecottage. These included individuals using the telecottage to access ICT, training and marketing services of the telecottage as well as those who did not use these services.

Approximately 80% of all telecottage managers stated that they were aware of other independent teleworkers in the local area, the average number being approximately 42. While most managers were simply 'aware' of other teleworkers, a quarter had established a skills register of such workers which was used to market the services of teleworkers to client organisations. One telecottage held a register of 500 potential teleworkers as a result of an extensive publicity exercise to advertise the services of the telecottage.

An average of 35% of workers known to managers had received training from the telecottage, and 76% were based at home. In terms of the use of the telecottage by teleworkers to access ICT and workspace on a full or part-time basis, approximately 37% of managers indicated having fewer than ten and 19% more than ten such workers. Telecottage managers indicated that the skills of teleworkers working independently of the telecottage were dominated by routine activities, and were similar in nature and distribution to those involved in work outsourced by the telecottage (Table 4.5).

The most successful form of marketing used by telecottage managers to publicise services to actual and potential teleworkers was word of mouth and personal contacts, with over half using this method. Other less successful methods were advertisements in the local and national press, trade and agricultural shows, conferences, viewing sessions and media publicity.

Table 4.5   The skills of teleworkers known of by the telecottages

Types of skills	Number of telecottages aware of teleworkers with such skills
Secretarial (word processing and DTP)	20
Software development and programming	6
Data input	6
Bookkeeping	6
Linguistics	4
Database management	3
Graphic design	3
Consultancy	3

4.6 Telecottage income and the future plans of managers

The quarter of telecottages established as private businesses gained all of their current income from revenue for services provided by their own business and/or by the telecottage. Thus revenue was predominantly derived from the provision of access to ICT hardware and training, but also from the provision of services such as word processing, DTP and more specialist functions such as computer consultancy. While some of this work was outsourced to local teleworkers, managers of such telecottages indicated that most of the work was undertaken by themselves.

The remaining three quarters of telecottages had received significant start up funding from public sources, with approximately two thirds still receiving such funding. While most managers of these telecottages indicated that income from outsourced work (as a brokerage fee to the organisations and/or teleworkers involved), and services (provided within the telecottage, such as ICT access and training) contributed to the income of the telecottage, only one in ten stated that they were now totally self-supporting.

Given these characteristics, many managers saw their telecottage developing in some way or another in order to decrease its dependency upon public funding. The main emphasis was on the development of teleworking and the telebureau concept within the telecottage - where income could be generated through training and marketing and ultimately through the brokering of commercial contracts for local teleworkers.

4.7 Summary

One aim of this research project has been to explore the characteristics of rural telework and to assess the extent to which telework facilitation policy is influencing its development in rural areas. This chapter has explored the characteristics of telecottages, which have been a result of such policy, and their role in facilitating telework across the UK and Ireland.

It has emerged that the telecottage is a recent phenomenon with the majority established in the 1990s and that most are located in rural areas. The most common type was the 'community business' telecottage, established by local public organisations as a community resource to facilitate telework largely through the provision of access to, and training in, ICT. There was only a small amount of evidence to suggest that telecottages were to any great extent creating new teleworking opportunities directly. For example, while just under half indicated that they were involved in outsourcing work to local teleworkers, the number of teleworkers involved was small and the work was predominantly part-time and low skilled. Moreover much of this work was being undertaken for small local companies, rather than large national companies. Although several managers of rural telecottages suggested that problems in securing large commercial contracts related to geographical peripherality and a lack of telecommunications infrastructure, the importance of word of mouth mechanisms in securing work meant that, while location was not a constraining factor in terms of undertaking telework, it was in terms of the marketing of this work.

It was also evident that telecottages were not important arenas for the day to day operations of teleworkers generally. For example, the use of telecottage workspace, training and marketing services by teleworkers was generally low. In addition, the majority of workers using the telecottage appeared to be involved in routine activities, similar to the types involved in the work outsourced by the telecottage. Given these issues, and the continued dependency of telecottages on public funding, managers were keen to develop the telecottage further, particularly in terms of the creation of a telebureau, generating income through the training and marketing of teleworkers, through brokering large commercial contracts for teleworkers.

This chapter has clearly demonstrated that telecottages are currently having a minimal impact on the development of teleworking in rural areas. While they appear to have established a link between themselves and teleworkers wanting to telework - through the provision of access to ICT hardware and training and also through establishing skills registers - the acquisition of tele'work', particularly from distant organisations, appears as yet undeveloped.

The following chapter explores in more detail the role, perceptions and experiences of those agencies involved in the establishment of telecottages and other telework facilitation strategies within the two rural case study areas.

5 The Telework Facilitators

5.1 Introduction

The examination of the role of telecottages in facilitating and supporting telework across the UK and Ireland in the previous chapter has provided a context for the next part of the empirical work. Here, attention is given to the role, perceptions and experiences of those public agencies and voluntary groups involved in facilitating telework and establishing telecottages in the study areas. It will be recalled from Chapter Three that preliminary conversations were undertaken with forty agencies and groups to establish which, and how, agencies and groups had been involved in facilitating telework within the two case study areas. This present chapter is based on in-depth interviews with 10 respondents from agencies which exhibited key involvement in telework facilitation within the study areas (see Table 5.1).

5.2 The background to, and identification of, telework facilitation strategies within the case study areas

Respondents in both areas indicated that their agency's interest in telework was in response to particular prevailing economic conditions within their respective areas and the perception that ICT may create new possibilities for local economic regeneration. However, it was respondents in Wales who emphasised most clearly the possibilities engendered through remote working as the main attraction of telework. It was apparent that such an emphasis related to the decline of traditional regional industries and the difficulties subsequently experienced in attracting investment to a geographically remote rural area:

> 'All the things that have been tried in creating jobs in rural areas have been things like building advanced factories, which doesn't work because they just stay empty ... [or] tend to import the workforce ... All the normal jobs in Wales are on the decline - coal, steel, agriculture, the wool industry, fishing, everything's on the decline. So unless you build advanced factories there is no possible way of creating jobs unless you create jobs by

Table 5.1   Details of the agency respondents interviewed and shorthand expressions used within the text

Agency respondents interviewed	Shorthand expression used within the text
Chairperson of Telecottages Wales (TCW) and IT Officer, Menter Powys	*TCW Chairperson/Menter Powys IT Officer, Wales*
TELEMART Project Officer and former Chairperson of Telecottages Wales	*TELEMART Project Officer, Wales*
Head of Economic Development, Powys County Council	*Head of Economic ·Development, PCC, Wales*
IT Development Officer, Development Board for Rural Wales	*DBRW IT Development Officer, Wales*
Business Connect Officer, Powys Training and Enterprise Council	*Powys TEC Officer, Wales*
IT Development Officer (Powys Telecentre Network), Powys County Council	*Powys IT Officer, PCC, Wales*
Telecottage Association Local Group Chairperson	*TCA Local Group Chairperson, South East*
Community Enterprise Manager, (Sussex Telecentre Network), Sussex Rural Community Council	*Sussex Rural Community Council Officer, South East*
Director, Sussex Enterprise (Sussex Telecentre Network)	*Director, Sussex Enterprise, South East*
Head of Economic Development, Chichester District Council	*Head of Economic Development CDC, South East*

encouraging telework. That way, you're not moving people and lorries around, but the people can work wherever they are. So even in the deepest darkest, most remote part of Wales, those people, provided they're trained and equipped, can be just as well employed as the people working in London, or Hong Kong or Cardiff or anywhere else ...' (TELEMART Project Officer, Wales).

Amongst respondents in the South East study area, however, it was suggested that interest in telework was a more recent phenomenon, originating out of the recession of the early 1990s. Whilst they were similarly concerned with creating new employment opportunities through telework, there was very little mention of the ability to work remotely as the main attraction. Rather, it was apparent that self-employed telework represented an alternative to the more conventional but declining employment opportunities available within the region:

'It's only since the recession that people in this part of the world have had to start thinking about other ways of [working] ... in this part of the world, in the home counties, easy commuting distance from London, people haven't really changed their way of thinking about work from the old traditional commute to London ... Whereas maybe through necessity, for people in the further reaches of Wales and Scotland, had to think about that some years ago ... A lot of people in the South East were [thinking about telework] because they found themselves redundant in the last recession ... A lot of people ... were looking for something to do following redundancy from a longer term career or job somewhere else, and I think maybe it's a necessity as much as intention to go teleworking as they weren't able to find another job ...' (TCA Local Group Chairperson, South East)

It emerged from the interviews with agency respondents, and also from the preliminary conversations undertaken with a number of agencies in both areas, that the promotion of telecottages represented the primary and often only policy towards telework by those agencies responsible for the economic and social development of such areas. All but one of the agencies interviewed had been involved in establishing and operating telecottages. Although telecottages represented a physical resource in terms of providing access to ICT equipment and workspace, respondents reported that most of the strategies for facilitating telework, for example training and marketing, were also provided via telecottages in the study areas.

Involvement in the facilitation of telework varied considerably between agencies in the two study areas. For example, the interviews revealed that there were a total of 19 telecottages in the Wales study area compared to seven in the South East area. Moreover, almost all of the telecottages in the former area were considered by respondents to be 'community businesses' - established and supported by public agencies as a community resource centre, compared to only two out of seven in the South East study area, the remainder of which were 'private business' telecottages.

'Telecottage networks', which aimed to give advice on, and to, telecottages and teleworkers, were also considerably more developed in Wales than in the South East study area. For example, in the former area there existed Telecottages Wales (TCW), an organisation with charitable status established in 1991 by local authorities and development agencies, to work closely with telecottages in Wales, engage in public relations and the marketing of activities of telecottages and to attract work into Wales. TCW also operated a membership service to provide advice and support for potential and actual teleworkers. Smaller, county-based networks also existed, for example in Powys, all telecottages belonged to Powys Telecottages, supported by Menter Powys and Powys County Council. Similarly, in Dyfed, SIMTRA was a network of telecottages established in association with the European Union DG VIII and Dyfed County Council.

Within the South East, however, telecottage networks were less developed. Although there existed the national Telecottage Association (TCA) established by ACRE and the RDC to promote telework and telecottages in the UK, its involvement with telecottages at the local level was minimal. Its main activities comprised producing the Teleworker Magazine and providing various national seminars on telework and telecottages. Despite the national focus, the TCA had been involved in recruiting voluntary individuals in each county to establish TCA Local Groups aimed at promoting telework and telecottages at the local level. Within the South East study area there existed four groups, one in each county, but such groups were voluntary and only one, based in West Sussex, demonstrated signs of activity in terms of facilitating telework. In addition, while Sussex Rural Community Council and Sussex Enterprise had been actively involved in establishing a Sussex Telecentre Network, at the time of the interviews the Network was in the early stages of development and had not been involved in any direct telework facilitation activity.

Although local authorities in Sussex had been involved in providing ICT training to small businesses, only agencies in Wales had been involved in any additional support activities specific to telework, namely training and marketing. For instance Powys County Council, Menter Powys and SIMTRA had all been engaged in providing a Telework Vocational Qualification (VQ) administered via several telecottages in Powys and

Dyfed. Also TCW, with funding from the Welsh Development Agency (WDA) and European Union DGX, had developed TELEMART, a project aimed specifically at marketing the skills of teleworkers in Wales to organisations.

The different levels of telework facilitation activity between the two areas reflected the European Union's Objective 5b designation given to this area of rural Wales. For example, many projects, including a number of telecottages such as Antur Teifi Telematics Centre and Bronllys and Talgarth Telecentre, telework training, for instance the Telework VQ and marketing projects such as the TELEMART project, had received substantial funding from European Union sources including LEADER, ESF and ERDF due to this designation. The South East study area on the other hand did not have this designation and as a result could not benefit from such funding and support.

It was apparent from this initial evidence that agencies had adopted a three-way approach to the facilitation of telework within their respective areas. These were providing access to ICT and workspace; providing ICT and telework training; and marketing and outsourcing work to local teleworkers. The following sections will now consider in more detail the activities and perceptions of the agency respondents with respect to these three areas of telework facilitation.

5.3 The role of ICT equipment and workspace provision via telecottages in facilitating telework

Chapter Two highlighted that the promoters of telecottages have reported that telework can be facilitated by providing access to ICT equipment and workspace to individuals wishing to telework but without the equipment to do so. This is also intended to support established teleworkers seeking specialist equipment or wishing to work away from home due to the problems of social isolation. In the South East, where interest in telework and telecottages was relatively recent, all agency respondents expressed a firm conviction in the effectiveness of telecottages in achieving these objectives:

'Also of course they're local to where people are, so it doesn't disrupt them too much to pop in there. And they can also use those facilities if they haven't got the capital to buy them initially when they're setting up business. You know, they may not have a fax machine for example or a photocopier, but they can pop down the road and get a quick copy done or a fax sent. And then as they get themselves established they will probably acquire the equipment themselves, but in the first stages they won't.' (TCA Local Group Chairperson, South East)

'[The] idea we had was using the resource centre as a business address for one man bands, so that people don't have to work from their kitchen or bedroom but use that as their professional address, and then all the services could be used from that facility.' (Director, Sussex Enterprise, South East)

Respondents in Wales, however, all of whom had witnessed the provision of such services through telecottages for a much longer period, were less convinced:

'... to some extent telecottages are old hat. Four to five years ago they were very innovative. The cost of technology was expensive so everybody tended to work and favour telecottages. And people have tended to move away from that to working as sole teleworkers ... and not necessarily attached to a telecottage.' (TCW Chairperson/Menter Powys IT Officer, Wales)

This quotation helps explain the low use of telecottages by teleworkers wanting to access ICT equipment and workspace, as indicated in the telecottage survey discussed in the previous chapter.

5.4 The role of telework training in facilitating telework

Agency respondents in the South East agreed unanimously that the provision of telework training via telecottages could help those intending to become teleworkers, despite such strategies being undeveloped in the area:

'Well I think [telecottages] can perform a very valuable role because essentially teleworkers would be individuals first and foremost. They will probably be inexperienced in some aspects of running their own business, probably inexperienced in the technology involved with computers, the Internet and e-mail and all that sort of thing. And telecottages like the ones I've seen locally, to me would be ideally placed to provide that sort of education at a reasonable costs ...' (TCA Local Group Chairperson, South East)

'First of all there's a target there of seeking or attracting people who are unemployed or who are wanting to return to work who are not in work at the moment, attracting them to a telecentre to train them with skills that would then allow them to set up their own business.' (Sussex Rural Community Council Officer, South East)

Within the Wales study area, however, training in ICT and telework was, as with telecottages generally, more developed. While most telecottages provided informal ICT training sessions on a piecemeal basis, more formal training sessions had been developed for telework. Of particular significance was the nationally recognised Telework VQ, administered through telecottages in Dyfed and Powys which aimed to train people in ICT and also in business skills to enable them to establish themselves as self-employed teleworkers. However, the inference that training in ICT could help individuals to telework was criticised by two agency respondents in Wales, the main remarks focusing on the fact that telework was simply a way of working and not an occupation. These respondents also considered that the Telework VQ failed to emphasise the business aspects of telework and the central requirement for workers to have a marketable skill in addition to general ICT skills. Ultimately, the extent to which learning how to operate a business remotely, as opposed to learning the skills on which to base a business, could help these people become teleworkers was questioned:

> '... teleworking is just a method isn't it? It's a way of doing a job, not a job in its own right. So again I'm critical of a the value of the VQ really.'
> (TCW Chairperson/Menter Powys IT Officer, Wales)

Subsequently it was suggested by one agency respondent, who had been involved in more general training for business courses, that anyone with the intention of establishing a teleworking business should undergo the same training as any other individual wishing to start a small business:

> 'It's the same concept, it doesn't matter what you're going to do, it's the same concept I'll put you through to actually start your own business up, because there are certain areas that you've got to do. Whether it's teleworking or whether it's ... if you want to survive in business there are certain things, disciplines that you've got to tend to first, and that's standardised whatever business you're going to run.' (Head of Economic Development , PCC, Wales)

Concern was also expressed by agency respondents in Wales about the skills and experience of individuals attracted to the telework VQ. Chapter Two highlighted that key attributes of the founders of information-based businesses have been the acquisition of particular marketable skills usually developed within previous employment. Two respondents suggested that the individuals creating a demand for the telework training have tended to be indigenous groups with an idealised view of telework and lacking such skills. Subsequently, respondents considered that these individuals were least likely to end up successful teleworkers, while potentially successful teleworkers were not likely to require the training of the VQ:

'The problem is you advertise in the press. That's what's happened - 'Teleworking NVQ', you've got Mrs Jones whose got nothing better to do on a Tuesday night basically ... just to do an adult education evening class ... That's the problem. I think if you look at the profile of a good, or what I would see as a good teleworker, you're probably looking at somebody that's quite academically sound. I mean, they're not your average farmer's wife. This probably sounds terrible but, you're probably looking for someone who has been in a fairly well paid job, and for whatever reason decided a career change, or they've been made redundant, which again makes a mockery of the VQ. You're trying to chuck that down the throat of somebody who can do that with their eyes closed.' (TCW Chairperson/Menter Powys IT Officer, Wales)

One agency respondent from the South East had similar experiences and suggested that a high level of ignorance about telework existed amongst those wanting to become teleworkers. He found that many of the people that had contacted him for more information on telework liked the idea of self-employed telework, but failed to grasp the fundamental business aspects of it:

'... I have been conscious of quite a few people who are redundant, out of work, maybe a business has folded or something and they are desperately looking for something to do, but they don't know quite what. And they get this rather rosy view of getting a computer and setting it up in the front room, and all of a sudden, work will appear ... The rules about setting up and running your own business still apply ... you have to have a skill, you have to have a market for that skill and you have to apply your skills to that market. If you can do it using computers and technology then you're maybe doing it via teleworking, but teleworking isn't the business, teleworking is the method.' (TCA Local Group Chairperson, South East)

Respondents in Wales were also concerned about participants' expectations in terms of securing work at the end of the VQ. Even one of the co-ordinators of the Telework VQ within Powys, who was generally in support of the course, expressed frustration about the lack of motivation amongst the workers. For example many on the course expected the co-ordinators, via the telecottage, to provide them with work. However, despite the common conception of the telecottage securing contracts for teleworkers (as highlighted in Chapter Two), agency respondents considered this to be more a responsibility for individual teleworkers than for the telecottage:

> '... people think that you're going to make it happen, [that] we as a local authority are going to go out and get huge commercial contracts. And again it's unfair to generalise, but they think they're better than just setting up their own business, they think they're special because they're teleworkers and we should really do more to support them. And of course we will as a local authority, and we can help with funding like the Brecknock teleworking group, but as far as going out and getting work in, you have to draw the line somewhere.' (Powys IT Officer, PCC, Wales)

Furthermore, it was stressed by one respondent that if people wanted to telework, they should, like most successful teleworkers, do it independently of the telecottage:

> 'I still say if you want to do teleworking, and there's opportunities there, then you've got to get off your butt and actually go and look for that work yourselves. And you've got to be sat at the end of the phone making contact with these companies.' (TCW Chairperson/Menter Powys IT Officer, Wales)

5.5 The role of marketing and securing contracts in facilitating telework

Despite the perception held by some agency respondents that marketing was a responsibility of individual teleworkers, agencies in both areas had been involved in establishing strategies to collectively market the skills of teleworkers to organisations. Although such strategies were relatively undeveloped in the South East study area, agency respondents considered them to be a main function of telecottages and telework support networks. For example, the TCA local group, which had been working with the Sussex Telecentre Network and several telecottages, had the intention of compiling a skills register of local teleworkers and subsequently use ICT to market these skills to remote companies wishing to outsource specific tasks:

> 'We are going to try and advertise through the Internet and those sort of new mediums that are available these days to try and get to potential employers who aren't necessarily in the physical vacinity, but maybe further afield.' (TCA Local Group Chairperson, South East)

It was agencies in Wales, via telecottages, who had been most active in marketing the skills of, and securing contracts for, teleworkers. Such activities to date had been on a piecemeal basis, with a small number of telecottages managing to gain contracts from remote organisations. For example, Antur Tanat Cain Telecottage had been involved in a contract with ICL processing data and Antur Teifi Telematics Centre had established a business services bureau serving local and remote businesses with translation and office services. It was acknowledged by most respondents in the Wales study area that the original remit of Telecottages Wales, along with individual telecottages, was to engage in the telebureau concept of marketing and securing contracts for teleworkers. However, two respondents expressed concern about how most telecottages in Wales had deviated from what was thought to be this original objective, focusing on the technological, rather than the non technological aspects of telework facilitation:

'The idea was, it was set up soon after Paddy [the former Chairperson, Telecottage Wales] had got this contract for ICL. And he said 'look, there is a tremendous opportunity to work and bring in business and we'll pass it around all the telecottages that are part of the Telecottages Wales as a group'. And the money went in to try and get somebody out on the road, to generate business. But that never happened, it became more of an Association that was just trying to promote technology and it was perhaps just the technologists rather than business people or people who could see the opportunity. So we didn't support it long term, in fact it got to a stage where they had got no money ...' (Head of Economic Development , PCC, Wales)

The lack of marketing and the dominant focus upon access to ICT training and hardware within telecottages was attributed by respondents to trends in funding. For instance, considerable European Union funding had been received for telecottages in Wales, intended solely for the acquisition of hardware and respondents were concerned that the funding had not encouraged the effective application of the technology:

'Part of the problem with all funding is that is has been all hardware related. All money that had come out of Europe - the majority of these telecottages, and the majority of the local authorities who have gone down this technology road, have been bumping applications to Europe for hard faced funding for kit, and that's great you know. There's millions of pounds floating around, and Powys is classic for this, if you want another computer, great that's great, but hang on do you need them? Hang on whose going to use them, what are they there for etc. etc. etc.? So I blame

to a certain extent the system. It's no use just supplying that kit, you've got
to teach people how to use that kit properly, and you know, buying 50
computers and putting 50 bums on seats to use them is great, but having
said that, it's sometimes better to buy ten, and spend that money on the
other 40 making sure that the ten that are using them are really ace.'
(Head of Economic Development, PCC, Wales)

Moreover, there was particular unease from two respondents about the
telecottages' reliance on income from publicly funded training courses
such as the Telework VQ. The respondent from Menter Powys, an
organisation which had provided substantial funding for the establishing of
telecottages in Powys, suggested that a culture of dependency on funding
for training and hardware had developed amongst managers of telecottages.
This meant that there was little or no incentive to find alternative sources
of income through, for example, the establishment of a telebureau:

'... that's when I get on my high horse really, none of the telecentres ...
actually get off their butt and do something unless there's public money
behind them to initiate that ... I think it's our fault to some extent, that
under LEADER 1, we were funding the creation of all these centres, we
gave them all the capital equipment. It's all capital projects it's never
revenue projects. So OK we've got these nice facilities in place, but like
the one down the road, and times are getting a bit hard, and they can't
afford to pay themselves, let alone produce marketing campaigns to
actually promote the use of teleworking, promote the teleworkers. It's
revenue funding that's the problem with the telecentres, the ability to push
themselves forward.' (TCW Chairperson/Menter Powys IT Officer, Wales)

Ultimately, it was felt by certain respondents that telecottages were now
non-innovative community ICT resource centres, replicating the services
provided by other agencies in the area, and failing to fulfil their original
remit of creating telework in rural Wales:

'I think telecottages have lost their way ... They haven't really got a clear
definition of what they are really about ... instead of identifying their own
niche in the market place, and concentrating on that. What they wanted to
do is spread their wings and become this all embracing agency that was
going to deliver everything - duplicate things that were already happening
out in the field.' (Head of Economic Development, PCC, Wales)

5.5.1 The TELEMART project

In 1996 a telework marketing strategy for the whole of Wales was established by TCW with WDA and European Union funding. It was called the TELEMART project and, according to the project officer, stemmed from a demand by teleworkers in Wales, rather than in response to the above criticisms:

'We had a meeting in April 1994 of our membership who are almost without exception self-employed teleworkers, and the big problem that they all identified was that there was difficulty marketing themselves. It wasn't any good advertising on the corner shop window.' (TELEMART Project Officer, Wales)

The strategy involved the identification of the skills of teleworkers who wanted to gain work through TELEMART. It subsequently involved the marketing of these skills to organisations who were identified as having key tasks which could be outsourced. Tasks intended to be undertaken through TELEMART related primarily to the skills of the teleworkers, but were principally non-specialist, involving advertising, typing services, presentation, production of manuals, exhibition services, travel booking, although a number of more specialist functions were also identified, such as translation, programming and market surveys. The telecottages were expected to act as central hubs from which work could be administered and outsourced to teleworkers.

Two agency respondents highlighted a number of key problems faced by the TELEMART project. The first concerned an issue raised earlier in terms of the characteristics of the teleworkers used to undertake the work. It has already been indicated that successful teleworkers have tended to have limited demand for the services of a telecottage, because they have the skills and means to establish themselves effectively at home. According to respondents, however, those who have been attracted to telecottages have tended to have limited skills and in some cases a lack of commitment to full-time work. Consequently, anxiety was expressed, even by the TELEMART project officer, about the quality of the workers to be used by TELEMART:

'We're looking at quality assurance because we've all had experience both as Telecottages Wales and telecottages of some client arriving with a large amount of work - you've written around to all these people that have been begging you for work and when you ring around - 'Oh well I can't do it at the moment I'm on holiday for three weeks next week', or 'I've got aunty

Liz staying with me, I can't do any of that', and one by one they let you down. And in spite of all the enthusiasm and all the, 'I must have work it's essential' ... and that's part of quality. The successful teleworker is always available, doesn't take holidays, works a 24 hour day, seven day week and that's it. And they appear to, they may not do, but they appear to, by the use of technology and the use of sharing work on, sub-contracting and so on. So I would always be disappointed if I rang up a teleworker and they say 'no', I would always expect them to say 'yes', and then find out ways of doing it.' (TELEMART Project Officer, Wales)

A second issue raised by two agency respondents was the way in which TELEMART was marketed to companies. According to the TELEMART project officer, particular tasks were to be identified, such as word and data processing, translation, marketing, which organisations did not already have in-house, but which could additionally be taken on and then outsourced to teleworkers:

'... we've identified pieces of work that they can outsource, that they don't have internally at the moment. We've made that condition, we said we don't want to take any of that work away from you, we are interested in looking at new work, taking on work that might improve your present performance.' (TELEMART Project Officer, Wales)

It therefore appeared that TELEMART intended to encourage companies to undertake additional functions rather than externalise functions currently held in-house. Considering the flexible labour use strategies adopted by organisations, as highlighted in Chapter Two, other respondents argued that companies would tend to downsize and externalise functions, rather than take on additional ones:

'... as TELEMART says, it's about creating new opportunities, new work areas within existing companies - I don't really think that's going to be the case. These companies are going to be looking at, as we said, to save money. If they can reduce the overheads of running an office in Cardiff by having ten teleworkers in mid Wales, they will close that office and use those ten teleworkers in mid Wales.' (TCW Chairperson/Menter Powys IT Officer, Wales)

Additionally, two respondents expressed apprehension about how the word 'telework' was used when marketing TELEMART to companies. They considered that companies would be solely concerned with the advantages of outsourcing rather than whether or not the work was 'teleworked' remotely from Wales:

'... you want to sell the case of basically how a company can save money at the end of the day. They're not concerned if it's a teleworker or a Joe Bloggs, as long as the company is saving money and still getting a good result ... It's going to happen, it's whether we're approaching it from the right direction is debatable. But yes we should be approaching companies first and looking at what elements, you know, preaching to them that you can save money by outsourcing, not by, don't mention the word telework.' (TCW Chairperson/Menter Powys IT Officer, Wales)

A fourth issue was highlighted by the TELEMART project officer and related to aspects of securing contracts from companies. The telecottage survey discussed in Chapter Four demonstrated the importance of word of mouth mechanisms in securing contracts. While the project officer recognised the significance of such mechanisms, he appeared perhaps over optimistic about the ability of TELEMART to establish a reputation which could develop within word of mouth networks:

'Everything is referral marketing, it's very rarely that you'll get a new piece of work out of the blue. I mean it does happen, it has happened, but it's rare. And that's what TELEMART is all about. We intend to make TELEMART a brand name, so that people won't be frightened - 'oh you use the TELEMART people and they were all right', 'yes they were good they performed on time ...'' (TELEMART Project Officer, Wales)

The final issue raised by two agency respondents related to the general strategy of TELEMART to approach only companies in Wales, rather than companies outside the country. It was thought that a central attraction of telework, particularly for agencies in remote rural areas, was the ability to import work and revenue into the area rather than simply shifting these components around the country:

'The problem was, that originally when the project was set up, the idea was you would actually approach x number of companies in your own area, your own country, Ireland in Ireland, Wales in Wales and whatever in whatever. But we were unhappy because there's no point in just moving jobs around a country, you want to get jobs into a country from elsewhere ...' (TCW Chairperson/Menter Powys IT Officer, Wales)

Given all of these concerns, this respondent appeared disillusioned with the ability of agencies to facilitate telework, particularly through the strategies employed to date. He reaffirmed earlier suggestions that successful teleworkers had little or no need for services offered by telecottages, arguing that in reality, telework cannot be facilitated through such initiatives, particularly when teleworkers targeted have tended to be those lacking the skills and experience required for telework:

> 'I don't think you can really [create teleworkers]. I mean you can say what are the benefits of being a teleworker in mid Wales - the environment and the ability to work as and when you want. You can promote the benefits and the disadvantages of being a homeworker, whatever. But that's really as far as you can go, then it's up to the individual to decide, 'Is that for me?'' (TCW Chairperson/Menter Powys IT Officer, Wales)

5.6 Summary

Chapter Five has explored the role and experience of agencies in facilitating telework in the two rural case study areas. Attempts to facilitate telework by agencies in the study areas have been based upon three basic strategies: the provision of access to ICT hardware, ICT and telework training and the marketing of, and outsourcing of work to, teleworkers. Telecottages formed the principal tool by which these services were provided to actual and potential teleworkers. Telework facilitation activity was considerably more developed in the Wales study area, primarily due to the Objective 5b designation given to these areas of rural Wales. As a result training and marketing strategies were relatively undeveloped in the South East case study area.

While agency respondents in the South East were confident that the provision of access to ICT equipment via telecottages could facilitate telework, respondents in Wales, who had a greater experience in this field, questioned the effectiveness of such initiatives. They argued that successful teleworkers have tended to work independently of telecottages due to the low costs of technology and the convenience of homeworking. Subsequently, they attributed the technological focus in the development of telework to the nature of European Union funding which has tended to be hardware orientated rather than encouraging its effective application.

In terms of the role of training for telework, and in particular the effectiveness of the Telework VQ, agency respondents in Wales criticised the focus of the VQ on aspects of operating a business remotely, rather than giving attention to how to establish a small business. They also reported that successful teleworkers already have the skills to telework, developed within previous, possibly urban-based, employment, whereas those indigenous groups creating a demand for telework training have tended to lack such skills and experience.

As for the telebureau concept, only a small number of telecottages in Wales had managed to secure contracts from organisations for local teleworkers. Indeed, respondents in Wales expressed concern about how TCW and telecottages generally have tended to focus upon technological rather than non-technological aspects of telework development and failing to engage in the telebureau concept. Whilst the TELEMART project in Wales attempted to address these non-technological issues, it was criticised for simply shifting low skilled work around Wales and failing to consider the organisational requirements and objectives of companies.

The present and the previous chapters have considered the facilitation of telework in the study areas and rural areas generally and it has emerged that central to the telework facilitation strategies of agencies has been the linking of the demand for, and supply of, telework, even if in practice this proved hard to achieve. The following chapter shifts the focus from the facilitation of, to the demand for, telework and considers the motivations behind, and experiences of, organisations using teleworkers in the study areas.

6 The Organisational Perspective of Telework

6.1 Introduction

Chapters Four and Five have highlighted the role played by certain agencies in the facilitation of telework, through the linking of the demand for, and supply of, telework, in the study areas and rural areas generally. Chapter Six explores the nature of the demand for telework through in-depth interviews with company and personnel managers from ten public and private organisations which have used teleworkers (also referred to as freelancers, consultants and independents within the text) in the case study areas (see Table 6.1). The chapter considers three key aspects of the use of teleworkers by the organisations; the motivations behind using teleworkers; the methods of recruiting teleworkers and the organisations' experiences of using teleworkers.

6.2 The motivations behind using teleworkers

It was acknowledged in Chapter Two that the organisational motivations behind the use of teleworkers relate closely to a desire to sub-contract work generally. Thus, while this section explores the decision of organisations to outsource work, it also focuses on the use of teleworkers specifically over other forms of sub-contractors such as larger enterprises.

Managers from both the public and private sectors were unanimous in their reasons for outsourcing work. These related principally to the desire to acquire particular, predominantly specialist skills not held in-house rather than the use of outsourcing as an overflow from clients' in-house functions. These motives related primarily to cost and organisational flexibility, as outsourcing enabled the acquisition of particular skills without having to take on the various office overheads and financial (such as National Insurance and tax payments) and contractual obligations involved in employing in-house staff.

Table 6.1   Details of the organisations interviewed and shorthand expressions used within the text

The surveyed organisations	Shorthand expression used within the text
Three Multinationals (with overseas offices), all based in the South East of England - one involved in electronics, one in electronic games products and one in translation	*Multinational, Games* *Multinational, Electronics* *Multinational, Translation*
Two National companies based in the South East - one involved in media, the other in market research	*National, Media* *National, Market Research*
Three County Council departments - one personnel department based in the South East, an economic development department in Wales, and an corporate IT unit in Wales	*County Council, Personnel* *County Council, Econ. Development* *County Council, IT*
One Training and Enterprise Council based in Wales	*Training and Enterprise Council*
One Development Agency based in Wales	*Development Agency*

This clearly allowed private organisations the flexibility to expand and contract rapidly in line with fluctuations in demand, as illustrated by the following responses:

'... it's actually a lower cost to us because if we had them in-house we'd have to pay pensions, National Insurance and all the rest of it, and they would be sitting maybe twiddling their thumbs. We don't know what languages and what specialist knowledge will be required of by our customers, so there's no point keeping a whole load of translators in-house with different languages in and out, when they might be sitting there kicking their heels.' (Multinational, Translation)

'Anything that is vaguely specialist we tend to contract out, because it's just not worth carrying the overhead internally.' (Multinational, Games)

For public organisations however, outsourcing was used to overcome the constraints of externally-enforced limits on their staffing levels, although the motives for placing such constraints originated from similar objectives:

> 'We use a lot of consultants because we're limited to the number of people that we can employ. So if we want, through our peaks and troughs if you like, that we have to use consultants to supplement the work ... and also to draw on their particular expertise in particular areas.' (Development Agency)

However, it emerged from the interviews that the decision of organisations to sub-contract did not necessarily imply a decision to use self-employed teleworkers. For example, five organisations indicated that particular tasks could be outsourced to larger companies as well as self-employed teleworkers. There did however exist a set of cost and non-cost related advantages of using self-employed teleworkers; for example, virtually all respondents indicated lower expense as the main incentive as differences in quality between teleworkers and larger organisations were negligible:

> 'I should think its bound to be price more, because it's the same sort of people but if it's another company they're probably going to work out more expensive.' (National, Market Research)

Furthermore, a similar number indicated that self-employed teleworkers offered a better service compared to that of larger enterprises, as one person was responsible for the task in hand, whereas in a larger company, responsibility was spread amongst a range of personnel:

> 'The advantage I would put to you is the responsibility angle. If you deal with one man, one man is responsible for it, sort of thing. With a multi-faceted organisation it's always passed around isn't it?' (County Council, Economic Development)

Other advantages cited by client respondents included increased flexibility and malleability in the working arrangement and the fact that dealing with one person avoided any mis-interpretations of the tasks required. These benefits are clearly illustrated by the following manager:

> '... if you deal with a large organisation you invariably deal with an account handler and [he] will come and take the brief and then he'll go away and he'll brief it to the person doing the work ... So you end up getting everything second or third hand ... [The relationship with an independent is] generally speaking more informal than a company and also

more malleable as well, in that if I need to do something at very short notice, they tend to be more malleable as it were.' (Multinational, Games)

While one manager considered a major attraction of using teleworkers to be the objectivity and originality brought to a task, the use of teleworkers in this sense also exemplified their vulnerability and dispensability to the organisation:

'As I said there is a hunger and a desire to come up with totally fresh ideas from freelancers because they're not bound within the corporateness of it all. So the freshness is the one advantage ... and it never gets stale because the second it becomes stale you use another freelancer. So there's a very strong logic to using freelance teams or independent teams.' (Multinational, Electronics)

While the use of teleworkers was generally considered beneficial by organisations, two managers from private organisations did express certain negative aspects of using such workers rather than larger enterprises. They suggested that whilst dealing with one person had its advantages, there were also drawbacks associated with this dependence:

'That's one of the advantages of the independent homeworkers, the personal commitment, and contra to that is that you get back up from an organisation that you don't from somebody whose working at home.' (National, Media)

These concerns did not relate to the lack of professionalism or quality on the part of the teleworker. Indeed, it has already been noted that most respondents received the same, if not an increased, quality of service from self-employed teleworkers compared to that of larger enterprises. Rather the perceived disadvantages related to the implications a lack of financial and institutional back up may have on the working relationship:

'The only danger is if they decide to think, 'oh I've had enough of this' and walk away from the business. As I say it's not happened touch wood, but it is a worry in that you have no recourse from an independent. There's no point in suing him because all he's got is probably his house. There's no reason to sue someone unless you're going to try and make money out of them. The risk is working with an independent who has no real tangible value if it all goes sour. And that is a comfort factor with a larger company because if it goes sour I can sue them.' (Multinational, Games)

Despite these concerns, only one manager indicated that such problems may actually militate against the use of teleworkers. While it was acknowledged by this respondent that teleworkers had their advantages, he indicated that if there was a choice between a teleworker and a larger enterprise, the latter would always be contracted to undertake the work:

> 'I do find that if you're using a one man band, you get a better personal service. What you lose with that is that when they go off sick, then it is a disadvantage and it weighs in the decision as to whether you put the work with the outworker ... If you know something is urgent, and you know that they are busy with somebody else, then it's a risk you have to take. Therefore the person has to have some very special skills. If it's 'even Steven's' between somebody who works at home on their own and a company providing the same services, you go for the company because of the back up.' (National, Media)

For most managers, however, the lack of back up was not an inhibitor to the use of teleworkers. Indeed, it was inferred by most that an individual's geographical location, office type, or workstyle was not of as much concern to them as the specialist skills they offered:

> 'It's the ... specialist expertise which is important. We don't mind where they work, whether they are home-based, or office-based or warehouse-based or whatever.' (Multinational, Games)

While the organisations' motives for using teleworkers related clearly to organisational flexibility, most managers appeared reluctant to discuss in the interview whether the adoption of these more flexible working practices had been preceded by organisational restructuring and the subsequent externalisation of functions within their organisation. For example, whilst four of the private organisations alluded to having periods of restructuring within their organisation, only two clearly indicated that restructuring and the reduction of internal staffing levels had preceded an increased use of teleworkers and sub-contractors generally:

> 'Of course, a steady reduction in headcount [has affected the decision to use independents.]' (Multinational, Electronics)

> 'Our business fluctuates a lot. It seems to be when the economy's bad we're good and vice versa, and at the moment we're on a roll which is brilliant, but it seems to be that when we've had to release staff, and some have gone and maybe not been re-recruited. When I first came [five years ago] we had a lot more, maybe 150 [people], and during the recession they

gradually went and maybe went for their own reasons, you know and we just didn't replace. We did have a slimming and trimming during the recession and a lot of ordinary people went as well as translators, so I can't say specifically.' (Multinational, Translation)

Although there was a small amount of evidence to suggest that the motives for using teleworkers had stemmed from periods of organisational downsizing, there was additional evidence to suggest that sub-contracting was also employed to accommodate individual motivations. For example, three organisations explained that the adoption of a sub-contracting policy enabled them to retain the skills of key workers who may have worked within, or in association with, client organisations, prior to establishing themselves as teleworkers:

'A lot of them, surprisingly enough, used to work within our own company and think right I'm going it alone, I can make more money and I can decide my own hours. So a lot of them come from within this company and other companies and they see a niche, and they'll set up.' (Multinational, Games)

'There are no people working independently that I use that I didn't use and didn't work with when they were employed or in another existence. They always came to my attention because they were a particularly talented individual working in an employed situation.' (National, Media)

'[telework] offers the greatest potential in terms of re-capturing or retaining highly trained, skilled people.' (County Council, Personnel)

Thus, while the use of teleworkers clearly offered distinct advantages in terms of organisational flexibility, the initiation of these more flexible labour use strategies did not relate solely to organisational restructuring, but also to the motivations of individuals wishing to telework.

Furthermore, although two managers suggested that it had been within the previous ten years that sub-contracting to self-employed teleworkers had become common practice, most managers indicated that freelancers and independents had been used for at least two decades - before the late 1970s and 1980s, which is widely believed to have been the period when many organisations underwent restructuring.

6.3 Methods of recruiting teleworkers

Evidence from the interviews with managers has demonstrated that key contacts and 'insider knowledge' have been important factors in enabling teleworkers to secure contracts from organisations. For instance within the large private multinationals in particular, methods used to recruit teleworkers reflected a relatively closed system:

> 'We get to know them, it tends to be word of mouth. It's very incestuous, the whole industry is very incestuous in fact. So it tends to be word of mouth that we hear of these people ...' (Multinational, Games)

> 'Typically we know them, but obviously we couldn't always have known them ... Quite often they're recommended so you might say to somebody, do you know anybody else that might be able to help on this particular job.' (National, Market Research)

Speculative marketing by unknown self-employed teleworkers was not seen by managers to be a very effective method of securing work, suggesting that, for workers outside the 'system', securing work could be highly problematic:

> 'Yes we do [get requests for work from other self-employed teleworkers] and we tend to turn most of them away I'm afraid, primarily because as I say it's a relationship affair ... I will go back time and time again to the same independent that I've been using in the past.' (Multinational, Games)

These responses also highlight the misconception that organisations are involved in a systematic process of competitive tendering, searching out best price for research and consultancy work. Rather the reluctance to use unknown workers and the reliance upon tried and tested workers reflected a desire of managers to counter the potential uncertainties and insecurities of teleworking relationships. This factor, in addition to the pressures of time, gave impetus to the closed 'incestuous' system:

> 'We tend to get lots of people writing in to us saying you know I've recently taken on a career as an independent consultant, after spending eight years working for such and such a company. Sometimes we see them but we don't have that much work to put out and we actually don't have enough time to try people out, so that's why it tends to be easier to go back to people you know and trust, as to say this is somebody new whose turned up shall we give them a go.' (National, Market Research)

The process of sub-contracting was, however, more open amongst public sector organisations, particularly for large contracts, which were subject to Compulsory Competitive Tendering (CCT). However CCT was often perceived to act against the interests of particular organisations who wanted to favour local businesses in order to support local economic development.

'It doesn't always go to the big boys. We tend to keep it so, if we can within the area, but there's Compulsory Competitive Tendering to worry about, and so I mean obviously things go a bit further afield unless we can get the numbers. One of the things I tend to do obviously in the business sense is to look for locals to supply, it would be criminal if we didn't, because obviously that's what we are here to do.' (County Council, Economic Development)

'... all Powys businesses ... are equally invited to tender for business. I don't say they're always accepted ... As I say they all have to go through the same procedure. So everything goes to tender. The large contracts by law now have to be sent out to tender ...' (Training and Enterprise Council)

6.4 The organisations' experiences of using teleworkers

Whilst organisations interviewed were sourced from teleworkers located in rural areas of South East England and Wales, these organisations clearly did not only use teleworkers in the countryside, but drew their workforce from various places in Britain and beyond:

'Oh we have freelancers down in Southampton, some in Dundee. So we have them at both ends of the UK.' (Multinational, Games)

'[Teleworkers] we use are located in] rural areas, but equally split between rural and suburban dwellings.' (National, Media)

'[Our teleworkers] are mostly within striking distance of London, there's one exception which is somebody we use quite a lot who's down in the West Country.' (National, Market Research)

'[Well teleworkers contracted are] located up and down the country.' (Training and Enterprise Council)

'Well [there's] one [teleworker] based in Belgium ... We have always had a large freelance database. I envy them because they move to Dorset you know, and they live there in a village in the country with all the benefits that's got but yet they're working with international companies like ourselves just because they've got electronic equipment.' (Multinational, Translation)

In terms of the remote working situation, all respondent managers stated that use of ICT in addition to more traditional forms of remote communication (such as the post and courier services) were central to the effectiveness of the remote working situation:

'[The problems with dealing with people at a distance are] less and less, and we're lucky in that we're a technology led company. So in terms of our communication we're pretty tight, but it used to be a problem when one had to rely on fax and stuff. I mean we will rely on e-mail and it's much easier. And I think one other thing you will find is independents tend to be technically quite well equipped primarily because they have to be, they all have e-mail, they all have fax etc ...' (Multinational, Games)

'Generally speaking we chat over the phone. Sometimes we'll have meetings and otherwise we tend to be faxing stuff backwards and forwards rather than e-mailing.' (National, Market Research)

'A formal, regular and effective communication system, whether written, oral or electronic is fundamental to effective remote working.' (County Council, Personnel)

It emerged from the interviews that the most important form of remote communication between client and worker was the telephone, as it was the only method where verbal interaction could be achieved. However, respondents felt that while they had their advantages, the use of remote communications, in particular telecommunications, could not outweigh the advantages of face to face interaction:

'[With face to face meetings] you can sort something out in 15 minutes that otherwise takes two days sometimes ... if they live in Cornwall or something like that. And notwithstanding all the advantages of improved telecommunications etc ..., the physical distance is often a problem, which you have to take into account. The counterbalance is that it's cheaper to work with these people than with corporations.' (National, Media)

'I suppose something is lost in telephonic communication, but they tend to pop in and bring work or whatever.' (Multinational, Translation)

Certainly, most organisations revealed that there was still a demand for close interaction between client and worker, of which face to face was considered essential. Consequently, some level of direct interaction with teleworkers was retained by all organisations. Inevitably, however, the often large distances between clients and workers impacted on the regularity of face to face contact and certain respondents found it difficult to ask workers to come into the office because of the inconvenience it would cause:

> '... it's irritating sometimes that you feel that you're putting them to some inconvenience by getting them in, and it shouldn't be like that, because one tries to develop personal relations with people who work at home. And you know it's like getting somebody out of bed, you don't do it unless you have to.' (National, Media)

However, as suggested, many of these disadvantages were negated by the development of personal relationships between teleworkers and clients. All respondents, for example, indicated that relationships with teleworkers were generally informal, often based upon bonds developed when individuals worked within, or when they had conducted work for, client organisations, prior to becoming teleworkers. Even within a translation company which dealt with hundreds of teleworking translators across the world, very good informal relationships were sustained:

> 'We know them all, they're mates, part of us. And it helps to keep them that way, because you know then we have a good personal relationship with them and then we give them the work and they are kind to us, and meet deadlines and so on. Oh yes, there must be a core of around 60-70 that are buddies.' (Multinational, Translation)

These informal relationships were considered by most to be advantageous in terms of reducing the possible negative effects of remote working on the relationship. This related particularly to the ability to 'put a face to the voice' when on the telephone. Finally, two respondents indicated that where high levels of expertise were being bought by organisations, the costs and inconveniences of regular face to face contact were an accepted part of the working arrangement, and as such were not really considered a problem by organisations or teleworkers.

Most respondents reported that due to cost and non-cost related advantages, the use of teleworkers at current levels formed a continuing part of their labour use strategy. Only one manager indicated that their use might decrease because it was a small firm with only four permanent staff and was in the process of expanding. Therefore, while all the other organisations had either previously reduced or placed limits on the size of their internal staffing levels, this firm had not yet established a core staff and thus when demand for a particular skill reached a certain level, it became cheaper to carry it in-house:

> 'We'll [probably use] freelancers less ... [because] I think it was just looking at the balance and saying hang on a minute, we spent £20-30,000 on freelancers in the year, now we could have had someone in the office for that sum.' (National, Market Research)

6.5 Summary

This Chapter has explored the wider structural influences on the development of telework and the general experiences of telework from the organisational perspective. It emerged that demand for self-employed telework has tended to be for specialist expertise beyond the capabilities of in-house staff, rather than an over-flow from organisations' in-house functions. The motives for using sub-contractors generally related to organisational flexibility and the ability to expand and contract their skills base in line with market fluctuations, without taking on the internal overheads or contractual obligations of in-house staff. The use of teleworkers over larger enterprises was linked primarily to cost, although additional advantages were considered to be the greater levels of responsibility, objectivity and responsiveness brought to the task by teleworkers. Problems with using teleworkers over larger enterprises related to the lack of institutional back up, which explains the premium placed by managers on informal and personal relationships with teleworkers. It was unclear whether organisational restructuring had, in most cases, preceded the use of teleworkers, as managers inferred that the use of teleworkers had been possibly going on before any periods of restructuring. Certainly, it was evident that the motivations of key individuals within the organisation to telework were factors in the decision of organisations to adopt such working policies. However, it can be inferred that organisational restructuring was of important historical relevance in initiating the use, by organisations, of sub-contracting more generally.

Whilst public organisations tended to have a more open system of recruiting sub-contractors, private organisations indicated that familiarity and reputation were the most important criteria for selecting teleworkers.

Rarely were 'outsiders', or those without any reputation or experience, used by these organisations. ICT was used to communicate with teleworkers located in Britain and overseas, although its use was regarded by managers to be greatly facilitated by personal knowledge of the person they were dealing with. Moreover, certain organisations still considered face to face contact with workers an important and invaluable form of interaction. Whilst the distances involved often militated against high levels of face to face contact, managers buying in the expertise thought that the financial and physical inconveniences of meetings were an accepted part of the teleworking situation. Subsequently, it was apparent that the geographical distribution of teleworkers appeared not to be determined or constrained by organisations.

Part Two of the book has given attention to the facilitation of, and demand for, telework in the countryside. Part Three now moves the focus of investigation to the supply of telework and examines the motivations, experiences and characteristics of individuals undertaking these new working practices in the study areas.

PART 3

The Supply of Telework

7   The Motivating Factors Behind Telework

7.1 Introduction

It was suggested in Chapter Two that, while it has been structural shifts towards more flexible forms of production that have facilitated the growth of self-employed telework, individual teleworkers have not been passive subjects in determining this growth. Indeed it was argued that individuals are active agents in these processes and an analysis of both 'structure' and 'agency' is required to make any coherent sense of this growth. Thus while Chapter Two and Chapter Six have elucidated the nature of these structural changes, this section focuses on the individual motivations behind self-employed teleworking in the study areas. More specifically, it explores the background to the establishment of teleworking businesses and the extent to which decisions behind telework have been influenced by a desire for self-employment, to work at home, to live in the countryside or combinations of these motives.

7.2   The nature of the teleworking businesses

Fifty of the 52 teleworkers had established businesses in a sector identical to that of their previous employment, suggesting that this employment had played an important part in determining the nature of the teleworking businesses. Table 7.1 indicates the types of businesses operated by the teleworkers. It was decided to use 'self defining' classifications on the basis of descriptions offered by the respondents themselves because official classifications, such as the Standard Occupational Classification, were not considered suitable due to certain practical inconsistencies. While some definitions were not precise enough, for example, with regard to specialist consultancies, others did not take into consideration the often diverse range of services offered by teleworkers, as with business and secretarial services. It is apparent that the majority of the businesses pursued by the 52 respondent teleworkers were 'professional', involving relatively high levels of expertise such as market research, journalism, translation and a range of consultancies. Furthermore, although most of these businesses relied on just one person, a number (particularly the consultancies and market research businesses), often dealt with issues of significant economic and strategic importance to organisations. Eight respondents, however, were involved in less information and knowledge-intensive businesses, such as business and secretarial services and bookkeeping. Three respondents ran telecottages based at their homes, two in addition to their business, and one as the basis of their business/secretarial business.

Table 7.1   Nature of the teleworking businesses

Nature of business	Wales	South East	Both areas
Market research/marketing	3	6	*9*
Business/secretarial services	3	3	*6*
Translation (Welsh and foreign)	4	3	*7*
Journalism/publishing	0	5	*5*
Computer consultancy	1	2	*3*
Training consultancy	2	2	*4*
Graphic design	3	0	*3*
Interior design consultancy	2	0	*2*
Medical report writing	0	2	*2*
Bookkeeping	1	1	*2*
Charity consultancy	1	0	*1*
Conference co-ordinating	0	1	*1*
Agricultural consultancy	1	0	*1*
European business consultancy	0	1	*1*
Public transport consultancy	1	0	*1*
Recruitment consultancy	0	1	*1*
Engineering consultancy	0	1	*1*
Accounting	0	1	*1*
Quantity surveying	1	0	*1*
TOTAL	23	29	*52*

The generally high level of expertise involved in the majority of businesses was reflected in the income generated by teleworkers, with over half characterised by annual incomes of over £20,000 (Table 7.2). A greater proportion of respondents in the South East were earning over £50,000, which can be linked to the concentration of teleworkers involved in very specialist businesses such as market research and consultancy in this area. Table 7.2 also shows the present income of the teleworkers ranked as to whether it forms a primary, secondary or equal contribution to the household income. Those involved in more routine functions such as business/secretarial and bookkeeping services tended to have lower incomes, in most cases supported by a larger income from a partner. It was also apparent that many of these routine businesses were a hobby or part-time and not critical to the financial well-being of the household.

Table 7.2   Present income of respondents and contribution to household income

Income level (£)	Total Wales	*1	*2	*3	Total South East	*1	*2	*3	Both areas
2000-4999	0				1	1			*1*
5000-9999	4	4			1	1			*5*
10000-14999	3	2		1	5	4		1	*8*
15000-19999	4		1	3	3	1	1	1	*7*
20000-49999	8		4	4	9		3	5	*17*
50000-99999	1			1	6	1		6	*7*
>100000	1			1	2			2	*3*
Refused	2				2				*4*
TOTAL	23	6	5	10	29	8	4	15	*52*

*1= represents secondary household income
*2= represents equal household income
*3= represents primary household income

7.3 The characteristics of previous employment, and its role in facilitating the establishment of the teleworking business

Previous employers of respondents in the South East study area were dominated by medium to large private companies such as SmithKline Beecham, Tate and Lyle, Interlingua, Philips, BP and various market research and advertising companies, with only one teleworker having run their own business previously. For respondents in the Wales study area, previous employers were largely public organisations (for example county councils, ADAS, universities and small charitable organisations) and to a lesser extent Small and Medium Enterprises (SMEs). Five in Wales had run their own businesses previously.

While the largest single group of teleworkers had established their businesses when they were aged between 30 and 39, over two fifths were older than this at the time of start up (Table 7.3). This implies that many had spent significant periods in employment prior to becoming self-employed. Furthermore, two thirds of all businesses were established within the six years prior to the study (Table 7.4), indicating that entry into telework by respondents was a relatively recent phenomenon with most making the decision to telework in the late 1980s and early 1990s.

Table 7.3   Age of respondents when business established

Age	Wales	South East	Both areas
<30	3	2	*5*
30-39	11	14	*25*
40-49	7	12	*19*
50-59	2	1	*3*
TOTAL	23	29	52

Table 7.4   Length of operation of the business

Years	Wales	South East	Both areas
<2	8	7	*15*
2-3.9	6	4	*10*
4-5.9	2	7	*9*
6-7.9	3	1	*4*
8-9.9	2	1	*3*
10-11.9	1	3	*4*
12-13.9	1	2	*3*
14-15.9	0	1	*1*
16+	0	3	*3*
TOTAL	23	29	52

Indeed, it emerged that all teleworkers had spent most of their working lives in employment prior to becoming self-employed. These periods in employment gave many the opportunity to develop specific areas of expertise, reputations and networks of client contacts which were utilised in establishing and sustaining their teleworking business. The 'incubator' role of previous employment, whether it was within a large company or a previously owned business, was critical in determining the nature and success of the subsequent business. For example, after the decision to become self-employed, most workers indicated that client contacts within the industry had provided the crucial starting point for their business:

'When I started, [my business came] through contacts that I'd built up during the years. So it's people I know personally ...' (Catherine, Journalism, South East)

'I suppose by and large I am exploiting a network of people that I knew from when I worked, when I had, what one would call, a conventional job which was about seven years ago. So quite a long time back.' (Max, Market Research, South East)

'Well basically it's personal contacts. Well I became self employed a couple of years ago, and before that I worked as a development worker for the Wales Co-op centre in Mid Wales. So I was known from that period of four years work, and previous work in this area. So basically it's the contacts I've built up over the years.' (Eddie, Market Research, Wales)

In over half of all cases (11W/19SE), support was given by previous employers and clients in the establishment of the new business. This was particularly so for workers in the South East study area, with around two thirds indicating that this was the case. Often such encouragement was in the form of direct business for the new enterprise from clients of the respondent's previous employer:

'All my clients moved with me, because my clients were Nat West and Royal Mail there. Not that they knew that I was going, I didn't tell anybody I was going 'till I resigned, and Nat West said, 'I don't think this should make any difference at all to us Kitty', which made me nearly die, I was so excited.' (Kitty, Market Research, South East)

This quotation also demonstrates how organisations have had to adapt in line with individual desires to telework, by adopting a telework policy in order to retain the services of key individuals. For around a quarter of respondents, however, it was the previous employer rather than clients (of their previous employer), who had actually provided work for the new business. In two cases such arrangements were accompanied by attractive severance terms during a period of restructuring within the company.

In all of these cases, 'insider knowledge' provided a competitive advantage over other enterprises and often a client base on which to start the business. Certainly, several teleworkers were clearly aware of the advantages they had over other businesses:

> 'In my previous business ... most of our clients were big banks and stockbrokers, and they've stayed. Because that's the nice thing, going solo is very difficult if you don't have the client base to start with, otherwise you have two years of void ...' (Neil, Computer Consultancy, South East)

Previous employment has therefore provided a crucial seedbed for the establishment of most of these small businesses through the development of expertise, contacts and reputations. These attributes were highly transferable and not closely tied to organisations and, coupled with low barriers to entry, enabled workers to leave established firms or previous businesses and set up on their own with comparative ease. Indeed it became obvious that it was such 'insider knowledge' that greatly facilitated the remote working situation, since markets and reputations had already been established in predominantly urban centres prior to establishing the teleworking business in the countryside.

However, several respondents involved in business/secretarial and bookkeeping businesses did not exhibit these attributes. Although they used the general skills developed in previous employment to undertake the business, they did not have any reputation or contacts within former employment to provide them with an established market for their services. Subsequently, they experienced problems accessing remote markets and establishing a demand for their predominantly routine functions.

7.4 Residential dynamics in relation to the decision to telework

A major consideration of this research has been an exploration of the extent to which telework is independent of the location of client organisations. It was suggested in Chapter Two that, because many small business founders spin off from former companies, regional industrial characteristics may shape the supply and demand for such enterprises. Subsequently, it has been argued that areas which possess an existing concentration of professional staff and large organisations were likely to exhibit higher than average formation rates (Keeble et al, 1991a). The research therefore intended to explore the degree to which telework was facilitating an in-movement of individuals into the countryside and thus a potential dispersal of telework activity away from concentrations of industry and commerce and into certain rural areas.

Table 7.5 summarises the residential histories of the respondents in relation to the decision to become a self-employed teleworker. Thirty three were still living in the same area in which they were based when previously employed, explaining the influence of regional industrial characteristics on the nature of the respondents' previous employers. For example, large private companies dominated the former employers of teleworkers in the South East study area whereas SMEs and public organisations dominated those within in the Wales study area. However, only a few of these teleworkers were indigenous to the area, and the location of teleworkers in the study areas reflected the fact that rural in-migration was already well developed amongst respondents.

Of the remaining 19 respondents, six had recently moved into the case study areas choosing to become self-employed teleworkers after a period of economic inactivity. Two of these were women who had moved with their husbands' work and three had moved into Wales with the intention of undertaking an alternative 'self-sufficient' lifestyle, but failing to engage in this way of life after their arrival. Thirteen teleworkers had moved away from the location of their previous employment and into the case study areas. Here the decision to telework was either accompanied, or superseded, by a residential shift into the countryside. For seven of these respondents, lifestyle preferences and the desire to live in a rural area were the main motivations behind establishing the teleworking business. The six remaining workers, on the other hand, had already started their businesses for other reasons, but took advantage of the spatial flexibility inherent in their situation to move to a more preferable rural location.

Table 7.5   Residential patterns of respondents in relation to starting the teleworking business

Residential patterns	Wales	South East	Both areas
Living in study area prior to starting the business	14	19	*33*
Started business after moving into study area	4	2	*6*
Moved to study area after starting the business	2	4	*6*
Moved to study area to start the business	3	4	*7*
TOTAL	23	29	52

All of these issues lead to a more detailed consideration of the actual processes and motivations behind establishing a business in the countryside. The following section explores in more detail, with reference to quotations, the motivations behind self-employed teleworking in the study areas.

7.5 The motivations behind self-employed teleworking in the countryside

It was suggested in Chapter Two that routes into self-employed telework have been based on two opposing logics of entry into more general self-employment. These have reflected two extremes from 'unemployment push' to 'self-employment pull' factors and 'combinations of opportunities and constraints motivating individuals to become their own boss' (Granger et al, 1995, p. 501). Although such factors were evident in the motivations of respondents to enter self-employed telework, it was clear that a simple 'self-employment pull' and 'unemployment push' typology was not completely adequate for explaining their decisions. In most cases, individual motivations to telework in the countryside did not come down to one sole reason, but to a combination of economic considerations, lifestyle and workstyle preferences, prompted by previous experiences and personal and employment histories. More specifically the decision to become a self-employed teleworker in the study areas was influenced by a combination of push and pull factors which related to the experiences and characteristics of previous (un)employment and the particular attractions of self-employment and homeworking in the countryside.

Despite the complexity of the decision making process, it was possible to identify groups of respondents which exhibited particular commonalities in terms of their experience of previous employment and also in relation to the principal reasons for becoming a self-employed teleworker. Subsequently, a typology was developed which reflected these commonalities. Its development considered firstly the question of what prompted them to consider a change of employment situation, for example whether they were re-entering employment, facing unemployment, or wanting a change of employment due to the perceived constraints of their situation. Secondly, it involved an examination of the principal reasons for becoming a self-employed teleworker in preference to more conventional employment opportunities. The following sections explore in more detail the motivations behind self-employed teleworking in the study areas, with reference to six 'types' identified.

7.5.1 Type 1 : 'Workstyle' (Seven in Wales and eleven in the South East)

This type comprises over a third of all respondents who chose self-employed telework in order to facilitate a *workstyle* shift and achieve greater autonomy and self-direction in the work process. Characteristically, these individuals left their previous employment voluntarily, motivated primarily by the perceived workstyle advantages of self-employed telework.

Often decisions to become self-employed were given impetus by the negative experiences of conventional employment, particularly for those who had been working in the South East prior to becoming a teleworker. Whilst the majority in this type were located in the South East study area, two respondents in the Wales study area had lived and worked in the South East before becoming self-employed. Dominant experiences related in the main to the negative aspects of working for an organisation and associated feelings of subordination, constraint and frustration within a corporate workplace:

'It was awful there ... if you left work on time, then everyone looked at you. I don't mind working a full day, but if I go in on time, I expect to leave on time ... I just hated the atmosphere, it was full of sloaney girls and they spent an incredible amount of time in meetings and doing nothing and writing reports about it. It just drove me absolutely nuts, so I left. And I intended to go freelancing at that point ... and I just think, I felt even then, I just can't bear the thought of working directly for someone ...' (Patrick, Journalism, South East)

Other push factors related to the pressures of working within strict regimes of management, control and supervision. This feeling was particularly strong amongst those who had been involved in journalism and secretarial work:

'You've got news editors breathing down your neck all the time, whipping bits of work out of your typewriter as you put the last full stop in. These were manual typewriters so your fingers were all battered. And there were a lot of things I didn't like about it. The fact that it was a daily newspaper, it wasn't like peaks and troughs of pressure, it was constant pressure all day every day, and the news editor actually had a policy of maintaining that. Like he was bringing in freelancers, he liked keeping everybody really wound up. So I don't think you can do it for more than a certain period of time really, you get burnt out.' (Gill, Journalism, South East)

'I was tired of working for somebody who can't appreciate you as a person. That's what I've found now, years ago no, but all of a sudden, all of the companies are changing their attitude. You're no longer a person, you're made to feel that you're lucky enough to be employed by their company, they don't think they have to pay you, they don't think you have to get any perks - anything you may have got that made working worthwhile years ago. And there was so many people higher than you, all fighting and watching their own backs, and it really is a rat race now, and you are just a number.' (Moira, Business/Secretarial Services, South East)

Conventional social and spatial patterns associated with employment were also given as reasons for wanting to telework. For instance, most teleworkers in this group had commuted to work in London prior to becoming self-employed and the logistical and economic disadvantages of this, in some cases, spurred the decision:

'It just seemed silly, when I first started down here, it took me two hours each way, and with a train strike it took me three and a half hours each day. So I was spending seven hours in a car each day to get to work. It just seemed a waste of time ... And I was forty, so I thought if I don't do it now, I'm never going to do this ...' (Kitty, Market Research, South East)

'... it was costing me an awful lot of money to commute. A half an hour train ride to Croydon, but it was costing me £1600 a year. And there was also the time wasted. Well if things were running on time about 15 hours a week, which very often ran to 25 hours, just lost, standing around waiting for trains, and I thought enough was enough really I can do this at home, I don't need to commute to London or to Croydon to do the same thing.' (Tommy, Translation, South East)

While all of the previous responses highlight the factors pushing individuals out of conventional employment, respondents were unequivocal about the attractions of self-employed telework. For example, adopting these new work practices offered an opportunity to escape the monotony of employment, venture into new areas of work, or to focus on one particular area of expertise:

'I suppose I just got fed up with doing the same thing, and I thought the life of a freelancer would be more varied.' (Mark, Journalism, South East)

'I think it was because I enjoyed doing a little bit of everything ... rather than commit yourself to one organisation. You know when I worked for Lloyds Lists all I was doing was writing about Zaps in the Persian Gulf, and that was about it. When I was working for Shell, I was doing their in-house magazine and that was it.' (Gill, Journalism, South East)

Interestingly, only a total of four teleworkers, all within this type, mentioned financial gain as a reason for becoming self-employed. This usually occurred when former colleagues, who had set up on their own, provided examples of the income that could be expected as a freelance operator:

> 'To be honest it was also better paid ... the freelance journalists were making more money than the employed ones and at the same time they got the freedom to work through the night if they wanted to. They didn't have to be in the office with somebody breathing down their neck at nine o'clock.' (Gill, Journalism, South East)

Six teleworkers in this type had moved into the study areas after becoming self-employed. Thus, while the decision to telework related primarily to the desire for self-direction in the work process, realisation of the spatial flexibility of their teleworking situation influenced a later decision to move to a preferred location in the countryside. For example:

> 'I'd been working in small campaigns for a long time and it was very workaholic intensive, long hours, very little pay ... It was mainly because I was exhausted and I wanted a complete change ...The move was partly because I'd been teleworking for a while, my wife's a further education lecturer, so our work was portable and we came to the conclusion that it would be nicer to live in the country, in pleasant surroundings than in London.' (Matthew, Charity Consultancy, Wales)

Distinct advantages of working at home were expressed by the majority of workers in this type; however the decision to work at home was in most cases not a primary reason for becoming a self-employed teleworker. Indeed, it was evident that for three quarters of all teleworkers interviewed, the decision was a consequence of the relatively minimal space requirements of the business and the low overheads sustained through working at home. This is illustrated by the following quotation:

> '... as far as I'm concerned, all you're really looking for is a desk, a chair a telephone, and ... a word processor, but if you can have that in your own home, and not pay 50-60-70 quid a week [renting an office], to me that's 60-70 quid I don't have to earn. So it cuts down on the running costs. I've never really considered working from an office, because I couldn't see any advantages. In fact I can see disadvantages ... One of the advantages for me is just being able to get on with work without being bothered about other people's concerns.' (Patrick, Journalism, South East)

7.5.2 Type 2 : 'Lifestyle' (Three in Wales and four in the South East)

While several respondents in type 1 had chosen to relocate to a more desirable rural area after establishing their teleworking business, the desire to move into the countryside was the main reason for seven *lifestyle* teleworkers to become self-employed teleworkers. Four workers had chosen to move into the South East case study area, three from London and one from Baltimore, USA and three into the Wales case study area, from Tokyo, Bristol and Birmingham. Three of these teleworkers suggested that their decision to telework was not influenced by experiences of previous employment, but solely by the negative experiences of city living:

> 'I used to work for an advertising agency in London, ... I decided I wanted to live somewhere like this, and then thought well what can I do with a job that enables me to live somewhere like this, because I wasn't prepared to commute to London ... I don't have to think about too much except my own preferences and if you think about it, well would I like to live in London working in an office, well not really, what would my idealised home be, and it's somewhere like this, an idealised home, therefore what are you going to do for a living? And that was the sequence in which it came. So I suppose it's about doing what I want to do.' (Max, Market Research, South East)

> 'We'd holidayed down here the year before, and I've intended to do this at some stage anyway, and it just got, ... city living was too much and I just jacked it in ... I resigned, 25,000 pounds a year and I just packed it in, and I came down here without a job ... I thought that the area could sustain me producing 35mm slides from my computer for me to make a comfortable living ... so I thought our lifestyle would vastly improve with the quality of life of the area and a nice steady income, picking and choosing the kind of work that I wanted.' (Phil, Graphic Design, Wales)

For the remaining four workers it was evident that a desire to live in the countryside was accompanied by an increasing animosity for their previous employed situation, whether within a company or their own business, and a subsequent desire for independence in their work. Thus, while they expressed similar negative experiences of employment to respondents in type 1, the spatial flexibility facilitated through self-employment was the main reason for choosing telework over other employment options. For example:

> 'I was on a very good salary but there was no satisfaction working for a company that had meetings four and a half days a week, and it suddenly

dawned on me that I wasn't the sort of person that could stand that ... literally, one week we sat in meetings from eight o'clock on a Monday to six o' clock on a Friday ... and I decided that if I was going to do it, I was going to do it my own way ... We had the place here and I've always been convinced that it is possible to run a business remotely, I know it sounds a bit big headed, but the salary that I was looking for, I was unlikely to find the right sort of job down here ... so it was either start my own business here and see if we can make it work, or move to London.' (Charles, Market Research, Wales)

For those who had run their own larger business prior to becoming a teleworker, the stresses of running a large business clearly prompted a desire to change direction. However, the decision to start their own teleworking business, albeit on a smaller scale, was mainly influenced by a desire to move to a more preferable rural location:

'Well the company had some problems, but nothing too desperate ... I was going to start a family and I used to lay in bed at night, thinking about clients, or do I have to fire somebody, do I make somebody redundant, it's just dreadful ... We decided that we wanted to change the structure of the company and it seemed like a good time to say right, time to do something different. I'd done 12 years of that and it was quite enough ... and we wanted to move to a more rural site, and becoming self-employed was an obvious way of allowing me to live where I wanted.' (Neil, Computer Consultancy, South East)

Although for three quarters of all teleworkers interviewed, the desire to homework was not a primary factor in the decision to become self-employed, two in this type mentioned that a desire to work at home in the countryside did influence their decision to telework. It was noted in Chapter Two that representations of telework have often reflected a juxtaposition of two lifestyles - living and working in a city, and living and working for yourself at home in the countryside. This was clearly reflected in the decision of these individuals to become teleworkers, as illustrated by the following quotation:

'... I found that I didn't enjoy office politics, I didn't enjoy travelling and I felt that my working life was cluttered up by a lot of things that weren't about what I intended to be when I wanted to be a journalist. So I wanted to detach all of that and just write ... Growing up in Croydon ... it's such a dump, and so many office blocks, busy, not particularly nice and then beginning to travel when I was a teenager and seeing other parts of the country and realising there were other ways of living ... And working in London as well, was pretty gruesome really ... I had always had this picture in my mind of living and working at home in the countryside and I had this vision of an office with a nice view, which is what I've got now.' (Catherine, Journalism, South East)

7.5.3 Type 3 : 'Childcare' (Three in Wales and seven in the South East)

Ten female respondents chose self-employed telework to facilitate spatial and temporal flexibility in order to cope with *childcare* responsibilities. Typically they chose to telework rather than to re-enter more conventional employment after a period of maternity leave and after deciding not to return to their previous employer. Typically the decision not to go back was influenced by the temporal rigidities of working within an organisation. Around half of these female workers would have liked to have gone back to their previous organisation, but they experienced considerable inflexibility on the part of the employer when they requested more flexible working arrangements to enable them to accommodate their childcare responsibilities:

'Well because of Robert, when I finished my maternity leave I decided not to go back to the bank, because of the hours ... I had to be there at eight o'clock in the morning and it would be six o'clock before I would leave, and so I wouldn't see Robert. I did ask the bank when I became pregnant about working from home but they said 'What? We don't do things like that here.' (Gillian, Bookkeeping, Wales)

'I had a child and I wanted to work more flexible hours. I wanted to carry on working but I didn't necessarily want to do a five day week, nine till five ... I took maternity leave and never went back ... I really wanted a part-time job, which was what I set out to find ... but ... companies were very inflexible in relation to people in general and women in particular ... but then [the company I was working for] were not willing to let me work three days a week which is what I asked for, which is a bit stupid of them because I would have probably put five days into three days anyway.' (Emily, Market Research, South East)

None of the mothers indicated any financial necessity to work since their partner's income was in excess of £20,000. Rather the desire to continue work related to the desire for the intellectual stimulation of another interest beyond children. However, the opportunities to re-enter conventional employment were constrained by the same reasons why many of these women did not go back to their former companies. Part-time jobs were considered flexible enough to fit in with childcare arrangements, but were regarded as lacking the levels of professionalism and intellectualism many of these women had previously enjoyed in their work:

> '... I looked at other part-time options, [but] there aren't really if you want to do what I think is a serious career job. Part-time jobs tend to be 'part time' jobs and I didn't want to do that sort of thing.' (Sara, Market Research, South East)

In addition, while the attractions of going back to work related mainly to intellectual stimulation, self-employed telework facilitated the spatial and temporal flexibility required to enable mothers to accommodate certain childcare responsibilities. Obviously, the ability to work at home was a main factor in the decision of all of these mothers to become teleworkers:

> 'I didn't want to be tied time wise and I think self-employment is the only way that you can be flexible enough to cope with days of sickness with kids or just days when you don't want to work.' (Eve, Market Research, Wales)

> '... with the bookkeeping you can be sort of like flexible about your time, because, well if something happens like say Robert's ill, well it's all right, you can either cancel the arrangement, or fit in doing it at home later on in the evening when he's asleep or something. You can work around any problems that occur then, if you're based at home. (Gillian, Bookkeeping, Wales)

7.5.4 Type 4 : 'Economically inactive in-migrants' (Four in Wales and two in the South East)

Type 4 includes six teleworkers who moved into the case study areas (for non-telework related reasons) and subsequently chose self-employed telework after a period of economic inactivity. Three had moved to Wales with the intention of undertaking alternative forms of income generation, including activities particularly associated with a rural lifestyle such as farming and running a small holding. This group reflects Day's (1989) 'ex-urban drop out' characterisation of in-migrants into areas of rural Wales - spreading into remote areas in search of alternative non-urban lifestyles:

> 'Well we decided to move, we fancied our chances of being, you know, back, not exactly back to the land, but you know, be born again hippies as it were. You know a plot of land, a few ducks and a few chickens and a dog, and a sort of old banger of a car, and god knows what.' (Laurence, Computer Consultancy, Wales)

'We both lived in London before coming down here. My husband left his job because he had a disk out of his back ... So he came down here and played with cows. I was in the Police and stayed working because we needed the money ... and then he got fed up living down here on his own, so he said, for God sake give up your job and come down, so I did ... we were going to keep beef cattle ...' (Andrea, Business/Secretarial Services, Wales)

In these cases, the decision to become self-employed came after such enterprises failed to sustain them financially and was influenced by a perceived lack of conventional employment opportunities in the local area. It also related to the attractions of being 'one's own boss', which was often more suited to their alternative philosophies of life:

'... eventually we actually moved, came here. We arrived and panicked instantly for about a week, realising how desperate this sort of situation was - how the house was and having no income. I had to sort of fight for social security, it wasn't an easy ride. And ultimately about six weeks after we moved, [a client contact] came up with the first phase of work, which has never seriously dried up since then ... So, the whole idea of the home spun, wine brewing, bread making, egg laying, you know, hippy, just sort of faded away into the background, and I became a home-based IT person.' (Laurence, Computer Consultancy, Wales)

'I think we thought that the pensions would give us perhaps a bit more money ... we're not very well off really ... Basically we're too old to get a job anyway ... I had a computer ... I'm doing a national diploma in computing and have enough equipment ... so we thought well we've got some knowledge why don't we get some work.' (Andrea, Business/Secretarial Services, Wales)

The remaining three teleworkers (all female) had moved into the case study areas so that their husband could take up a new job and indicated how a lack of alternative opportunities locally was a catalyst to the decision to become self-employed:

'Well I hoped to get a job of a similar nature with a college or with local government ... I did make a conscious decision not to apply for anything which didn't interest me or didn't pay enough ... as I hadn't got a job, and was finding it difficult to get one, I thought that this was another route to look at.' (Sophie, Business/Secretarial Services, Wales)

'Basically when we moved [to Surrey] ... there were no pharmaceutical companies within commuting distance, so I thought right I'll give it a try

... I could have tried to get a job with Wellcome who I suppose would have been about three quarters of an hour's journey away. I did think about that, I did think about doing something completely different.' (Beth, Medical Report Writing, South East)

7.5.5 Type 5 : 'Threat of unemployment' (One in Wales and two in the South East)

Three teleworkers chose self-employment in response to a perceived *threat of unemployment* during times of organisational restructuring within their organisation. Rather than be forced out with no other options, they made alternative arrangements prior to any change. Although they did consider re-entering conventional employment, various factors encouraged them to become self-employed. For example, one respondent's decision was prompted by the limited demand for his skills within conventional employment opportunities locally:

'I was employed with the Dyfed County Council translation unit, ... re-organisation was looming, and is still looming ... and I didn't foresee the new unitary authority employing more than perhaps two. So that was the prime consideration. At that time there weren't too many jobs being advertised for translators in this area. We don't want to move from this area ... I was young enough to venture, and old enough to have gained experience in the field and also just wanted to give it a try.' (Ivor, Translation, Wales)

The two others in this type were offered attractive severance terms by employers at times of organisational restructuring. As such, the considerable financial packages given to these workers, in addition to the offer of sub-contracted work from ex-employers and clients, meant that the transition into self-employment was a more appealing and appropriate option than attempting to re-enter conventional employment:

'... well I played the three card trick, I made myself redundant, walked away with a big pot of gold, and big pension - served 33 years in BP and then outsourced myself back to them as a consultant and so about 90 days work a year for BP ... Well it was in keeping with the general trend in BP, in that they don't like bodies on the payroll, so they were getting rid of people and outsourcing as many skills as possible, to buy them in as and when they require them rather than have a body on the pay roll.' (Percival, Engineering Consultancy, South East)

7.5.6 Type 6 : 'Forced unemployment' (Five in Wales and three in the South East)

This final type includes eight individuals who had chosen self-employed telework after being *forced into unemployment* through redundancy or business collapse. Those in the South East were typically made redundant by large multinationals, including SmithKline Beecham and IBM. In Wales, three of the respondents were forced into unemployment through the collapse of a previously owned SME and two through redundancy from an SME and ADAS. All three workers in the South East attempted to find new employment, but there was often considerable aversion to having to rejoin another organisation at the bottom of the career ladder:

> 'I did go for one job interview, but I really couldn't get enthusiastic about that ... I was on the lower rungs of management and felt that ... I would have to start right at the bottom again. And when you get to your mid forties, that's difficult. I didn't want to take on a too junior role.' (Jenny, Medical Report Writing, South East)

Those in the Wales study area, however, made only limited attempts to seek out alternative employment. The lack of demand in Wales for their specific skills within conventional employment meant that the only realistic option was to establish their own business:

> 'I had a good handout from ADAS when I left. I looked for a job, but I have never found anything that I am qualified for, or wanted to do. I spent six months prior to setting up in business half-heartedly looking through the summer, but then decided that I know what I'm good at, so I decided that I would give it a go with the provision that the money that I had got would support us for probably three or four years if absolutely necessary.' (Adrian, Agricultural Consultancy, Wales)

> 'I got made redundant, and ... I virtually went self-employed immediately because I knew that I would never get a job again, not around here, and especially not like the one I had, I just knew. I like typesetting and I'm good at it, and you know, I'm not really very good at anything else, and so, I just wanted to do that.' (Rose, Graphic Design, Wales)

For those who had previously run their own businesses, restarting a business, albeit on a smaller scale, seemed a more natural progression into employment than seeking a conventional position with an organisation. Certainly, it appeared that for these respondents the negative experiences of operating a large business actually influenced their desire to establish a small, single person business with low overheads and minimal financial risks:

> 'We had premises, we had staff and all sorts of things, we had a load of problems in the recession. The problem is that if you have got a lot of staff, that is a fixed overhead, and whether the business is coming on or not, you have still got to cope with that fixed overhead ... so I set up something simple' (Irvin, Interior Design Consultancy, Wales)

> 'In the early nineties we were a victim of the recession, and we went into receivership ... I mean I really enjoyed the print so I decided to set up doing pre-press side of things.' (Rob, Graphic Design, Wales)

7.6 Summary

This chapter has given attention to the factors underpinning the decision of individuals to become self-employed teleworkers in the two study areas. It emerged that previous employment played an important role in facilitating the teleworking situation. For example, expertise, reputation and networks of client contacts developed within former employment were essential to the successful establishment of the business and greatly facilitated the remote working situation, as markets and reputations had already been established in predominantly urban centres prior to deciding to telework in the countryside. These factors meant that most individuals could set up teleworking businesses with comparative ease. Certainly, there was limited evidence pointing to the development of indigenous telework activity and the existence of successful teleworking operations in the study areas had largely been determined by the residential preferences and dynamics of teleworkers.

Reluctant or enforced self-employment as a consequence of redundancy or business collapse, stimulated the establishment of relatively few businesses. In addition, although a few respondents were re-recruited on a sub-contract basis by former employers after deciding to telework, none were forcibly unemployed, suggesting that formal externalisation was not a major factor prompting workers in the study areas into telework. Nearly half of all respondents, on the other hand, actually made an independent and positive decision to become self-employed teleworkers rather than remain in employment. Various push factors related to the animosity of city living and the experiences of former employment, whether within a large organisation or in one's own large business. Attractions of self-employed telework included the desire to achieve greater freedom, flexibility and scope, not only in their working arrangements but also in their lifestyle and residential patterns. For example, while several had moved to a more rural location after becoming teleworkers, a similar number actually chose telework solely to facilitate a residential shift to the countryside. Clearly telework in this context represents a counter-culture, not only against the corporate nature of organisations through the desire to work independently of them, but also in response to urbanism, in the decision of a number of respondents to relocate to the countryside, from largely urban areas.

Although just over a third of teleworkers had entered self-employment after a period of economic inactivity, their entry was voluntary and the positive attractions of telework, for example spatial and temporal flexibility, accompanied by the perceived constraints of conventional employment in terms of characteristics and availability, influenced their decision. The lack of alternative employment opportunities in the Wales study area was a particularly dominant factor influencing the decisions of these individuals to telework.

As for homeworking, although certain respondents, predominantly mothers, were attracted to self-employed telework because of the ability to work at home, many of the other teleworkers did not consider homeworking to be a main motivating factor. Rather the decision to work at home was simply a consequence of the minimal spatial requirements of the business and minimal overheads incurred through homeworking.

While this chapter has considered the factors influencing the decision of individuals to become self-employed teleworkers, the following chapter shifts the emphasis to the characteristics and dynamics of the teleworking situation and in particular the extent to which telework is independent of the location of client organisations.

8 The Characteristics and Dynamics of Telework

8.1 Introduction

While Chapter Seven focused on the initial motivations behind self-employed telework in the study areas, this chapter is concerned with the characteristics and dynamics of telework. It was suggested in Chapter Two that while developments in ICT have enabled particular information-based services to be provided remotely, such spatial independence may be moderated by the requirement of these businesses to interact closely with clients. Such arguments raise important questions as to the extent to which telework can be undertaken for markets beyond the local area and, more specifically, the degree to which remote communications have replaced the need for face to face contact in communicating with, and securing contracts from, organisations. This chapter explores these issues by focusing on the characteristics of the teleworkers' clients; the methods by which teleworkers secure work and communicate with clients; the external perceptions of teleworkers; and the extent to which telecottages are an integral part of the teleworking situation.

8.2 The nature of the teleworkers' clients

It was suggested earlier that not all self-employed individuals, particularly those based at home, conform to the liberal definition of self-employment since they are quasi-employees working for one organisation while being formally self-employed because of cost advantages accrued to the employer. However, evidence from this study indicates that the vast majority of respondents could be considered to be running their own businesses, as opposed to quasi-employees, as over nine out of ten teleworkers interviewed were working for multiple clients (Table 8.1).

Table 8.1   **Number of clients considered 'regular' or 'frequent' by respondents**

No. of regular or frequent clients	Wales	South East	Both areas
1	1	2	*3*
2-5	4	13	*17*
>5	18	14	*32*
TOTAL	23	29	*52*

Although several teleworkers had long-term retainers with companies, the majority had verbal or written contracts ranging from a couple of hours to one year. The nature of contracts undertaken was determined by the respondent's business; for instance, translators typically worked on several different documents each day and charges were made for each page translated. For market researchers and other consultants, contracts were usually on a project basis and lasted for longer periods from one month to one year.

It was evident from the interviews that respondents worked for multiple clients located at a variety of spatial levels. However, an attempt to gain an impression of the extent of remote working was achieved by asking teleworkers to indicate their most distant client, whether past or present. Around nine out of ten respondents had dealt with clients beyond the local level, with nearly two thirds indicating that these clients were based at national and international levels (Table 8.3). A greater proportion of teleworkers in the Wales case study area had only served local clients, whilst in the South East, a much higher proportion had worked for organisations located in Europe and further afield.

Table 8.2   **Location of respondents' most distant client**

Location of client	Wales	South East	Both areas
International (outside Europe)	2	6	*8*
European (within Europe but outside UK)	1	4	*5*
National - beyond 80 miles (but within UK)	11	9	*20*
Regional - between 20-80 miles	4	9	*13*
Local - less than 20 miles	5	1	*6*
TOTAL	23	29	*52*

Despite evidence of the interregional and international exchange of work, examination of the teleworkers' total client base reveals that regional influences were still apparent in terms of the concentrations of client sectors served. The concentration of 'blue chip' national and multinational organisations involved in both the manufacturing and service sectors in the South East area generally was reflected in the dominance of these sectors amongst the clients of respondents in this area. The dominance of SMEs and the public sector within the Welsh economy was similarly reflected in the client base of workers in the Wales study area. Teleworkers involved in routine functions such as secretarial and business functions tended to serve only local SMEs.

Two sets of respondents in both areas, however, exhibited particular concentrations of national as well as overseas clients. The first consisted of those who had moved into the case study areas, away from the location of their client contacts and sources of work. Lloyd, for example, had moved to Reigate from the USA, where his previous employer and major clients were located and Edmund had moved into rural Wales from Japan where he had established a network of clients for his Japanese translation checking service.

The second set comprised those individuals involved in foreign language translation. Although the nature of the international translation business meant, by its very nature, that clients were international, the location of translation agencies which were the main clients of translators was particularly dispersed, as they had adapted both organisationally and technologically to deal with independent teleworking translators located across the world. Mechanisms for supplying and receiving work were therefore heavily orientated towards the use of ICT, such as the fax or modem, rather than face to face interaction.

8.3 Communicating with clients

8.3.1 Methods used to communicate remotely with clients

As nearly two thirds of all respondents had been involved in markets located at national and international levels, it was anticipated that the use of remote communications would be central to the maintenance of effective working arrangements, as found within the interviews with organisations, discussed in chapter six. While the use of more advanced telecommunication technologies such as modems had been considered central to the effectiveness of telework, some commentators have argued that more traditional forms, such as the use of courier services to send disks, are similarly effective (Kinsman, 1987, Korte, 1988, Lewis, 1988). It was therefore expected that respondents might also rely upon more conventional forms of communication, as well as more advanced telecommunications technologies to communicate work.

Table 8.3   Methods of remote communication used by teleworkers

Methods used	Wales	South East	Both areas
Telephone	23	29	*52*
Fax	15	24	*39*
Post/courier	14	14	*28*
Modem	8	10	*18*

By definition, all teleworkers used a computer when undertaking their work. Table 8.3 shows the methods employed by teleworkers to communicate with clients. Unsurprisingly, the telephone was used by all those interviewed to communicate verbally with clients. The fax was the most widely used method for the physical transfer of work, being used by three quarters of respondents. The use of post and courier services was also widespread, with over half of all respondents using these more traditional methods. The modem was only used by about a third of all teleworkers.

It was apparent that particular methods of communication were used for different purposes. For example, the fax and the phone were used for more informal communication such as discussing work and generally keeping in touch. The modem and courier services, on the other hand, were used for sending more formal documents such as final reports and large texts. The levels of use of these methods of communication were determined by the degree of client interaction required for the respondent's business. For certain businesses, such as translation, report writing and journalism, the majority of the work could be undertaken in relative isolation, requiring little interaction with clients. Communication, usually in the form of sending and receiving documents, was only required at the beginning and end of the task, as illustrated by the following response:

'They ring you up and say 'I've got so many pages or x number of words in whatever language it is, can you do it by such and such a date?', and you say 'yes' or 'no'. It normally comes by fax, it depends. If it's up to 10 pages it will come by fax, if it's a large document, I normally tell them to fax me a dozen pages and send the whole thing in the post, and that gives me work to get on with and the next day I can do the rest of it ... I have a modem, I use that for sending jobs out.' (Tommy, Translation, South East)

For consultancy and market research, however, the requirement for more intensive informal client interaction was greater, usually involving extensive use of the telephone and the fax to discuss the work:

'I communicate with clients on the phone and by fax. The phone's ringing all the time. You've got your clients feeding you with information and then you're contacting people ...' (Emily, Market Research, South East)

In terms of the standard physical transfer of information (for example, documents and reports), many respondents still used the post and courier services to send information to clients (by disk and/or hard copy). Several respondents, including those working in remote areas of rural Wales, stated that this method was as effective for sending information as using a modem:

'I send stuff to Washington by DHL [couriers]. That's quite impressive, I ring up DHL up to 10pm at night here [in the Brecon Beacons] and they will collect before mid-day.' (Matthew, Charity Consultancy, Wales)

Moreover, one teleworker suggested that the use of the post was perhaps a more effective method of sending information than by modem, because text in hard format was more manageable than data sent to a computer:

'I don't need a modem, because if somebody wants a report in a month, the fact that I can't send it down the line is neither here nor there. In fact most of the people I work with are under very heavy pressure in their own offices, so the last thing they want is a damn report coming down the line. It's far more manageable from their point of view if I send them a report by post, they can put it to one side for a day or two, read it at leisure and get back to me.' (Eddie, Market Research, Wales)

The reliance upon these more traditional forms of remote communication did not reflect a lack of technological expertise amongst respondents. Rather, several considered that, despite their acquisition of advanced ICT, its use was constrained by the technological limitations of client organisations:

'I think quite often individual self-employed people, teleworkers whatever you want to call them, like myself, find that we have much more advanced hardware and software than our clients, which in a sense is opposite to what you might expect, and leads to quite considerable difficulties in transferring files, information and access and stuff.' (Matthew, Charity Consultancy, Wales)

Particular respondents, however, were working in client sectors, such as translation and computer consultancy, which were heavily reliant upon the use of more advanced telecommunications technology because they had adapted both organisationally and technologically to deal with many teleworkers. Indeed, certain translators exhibited quite impressive working methods. For example, Edmund had set up a translation checking service while teaching in Japan before moving to rural Wales:

'They send the work using a local call to a node which is connected to a computer in Tokyo, and I access that computer from here. I just check it about three o'clock, I'll go and see if there's anything there. If there is then I start writing.' (Edmund, Translation, Wales)

8.3.2 Levels of face to face contact between clients and teleworkers

Despite the considerable use of remote communications by teleworkers, the interviews revealed that most still found it necessary to interact with clients on a face to face basis. This was particularly so amongst specialist businesses, such as market research and consultancy, where specific expertise was being purchased by the client:

'The people I work regularly for I see them more regularly because they tend to use me as a proper consultant, in other words, they pick my brain ...' (Emily, Market Research, South East)

'... in this business, what clients are buying is you as an individual, and therefore you have to meet them on a personal level ...' (Laura, European Business Consultancy, South East)

An additional reason given for maintaining face to face interaction was the ability to read the particular interpersonal messages of clients, which could not be achieved through the telephone or other forms of remote communication:

'I do see clients face to face, and that's fairly important that you do keep in touch with people on a personal level because, I think perhaps sometimes if things aren't going quite right, you might not know quickly on the phone, whereas, if you're sitting face to face you gain that impression. I think that's quite important.' (Evelyn, Journalism, South East)

Respondents with concentrations of clients within the region exhibited quite high levels of face to face contact with clients, facilitated by their proximity to them. However certain teleworkers had concentrations outside of the region, and although for those in the translation sector, the requirement for face to face interaction was not high, for others providing specialist consultancy, direct interaction was, as indicated above, an important part of the client - teleworker relationship. Even so, in most of these cases, direct interaction with clients was maintained, despite the often considerable distances and costs involved. For example, Charles, a consultant living in the Brecon Beacons, Wales, spent at least half of his time 'zipping round the country' visiting clients. Indeed, Thrift (1994) has suggested that the intense use of telecommunications by businesses, and increasing levels of information communicated internationally, may lead to an increased, not decreased use of face to face contact in order to decipher and make sense of such information. Such a trend was highlighted by Charles:

'Yes, yes, I think it was Boeing who did an advert a few years ago that said, 'there's nothing quite like shaking hands', and really they were saying the world is becoming smaller with faxes and with Internet and all that type of activity, that there's nothing quite like seeing the guy.' (Charles, Market Research, Wales)

8.4 Methods of acquiring clients

It was demonstrated in the previous chapter that, for the majority of respondents, the most important method of acquiring initial contracts for the business was through networks of client contacts developed in previous employment. This helps explain the concentration of regional clients served by many respondents, as about two thirds had not moved away from the area in which they had previously worked. The interviews with teleworkers also revealed that this 'insider knowledge' greatly facilitated the remote working situation, both for those with regional, as well as national and overseas clients, as markets and reputations had already been established in predominantly urban centres prior to setting up the teleworking business in the countryside.

For the majority of teleworkers, the development of new clients was dependent upon the growth and renewal of specialist expertise and reputations, focused on expanding markets through the evolution of client contacts. This had the effect of increasing concentrations of clients in particular markets and locations, as new clients evolved from old ones.

Rarely were large amounts of work secured from traditional methods of marketing such as mail-shots, cold calling and advertising:

> 'Recommendation, previous good experience, that's the majority of our business, and it's networking, contacts, that sort of stuff. I think small businesses, particularly the ones who work from home, tend to work best from that, because it's very difficult to target our type of customer, you can't do it through advertising.' (Charles, Market Research, Wales)

> '... things evolve. I think my first clients were people who knew me, who I'd worked with, but then you get say, for example, you get a project through an advertising agency for one of their clients, well then that client may employ me directly. Or somebody who I know moves on to a new job, they ring me up from their new place.' (Max, Market Research, South East)

However, it was highlighted in Chapter Seven that a few teleworkers had established businesses not closely connected to previous employment, and as such could not benefit from the previous reputations and networks of client contacts, enjoyed by the majority of other teleworkers. These businesses involved predominantly routine services such as secretarial/business services and were founded largely upon the misplaced notion that the acquisition of ICT could enable them to telework. Indeed, one of the respondents called her business a telecottage, without it really conforming to what would normally be considered a telecottage. Inevitably, the businesses of these workers were constrained by non-technological factors, such as problems accessing remote urban markets, difficulties establishing clients with no reputation or contacts in the industry and, perhaps most importantly, problems establishing a demand for their basic, routine services such as word processing. Often their perceptions of telework were naive, linking it with a type of job as opposed to a way of undertaking a particular service:

> 'We're not really sure how we go about getting work. I mean whether we write to customers, BP and all these big firms and say we're teleworkers, can we have a contract, you know?' (Sonia, Business/Secretarial Services, Wales)

Despite the lack of professional contacts however, these respondents indicated that the work they had secured had come from social networks and contacts, such as friends and business colleagues of partners:

'All the jobs we have got at the moment are from personal contacts.'
(Andrea, Business/Secretarial Services, Wales)

'I got the work because my husband knew the person and he was looking
for someone at the time and just passed it on to me.' (Moira,
Business/Secretarial Services, South East)

However, the routine nature of much of their work, in conjunction with the
lack of reputation and networks of client contacts, meant that the client
base of these respondents tended to be local small businesses.

Interestingly, one Welsh-speaking respondent indicated that the
existence of more close-knit social and business networks within the Welsh
speaking community provided additional advantages in terms of securing
work:

'The Welsh networking is much more incestuous than normal networking.
We have just got the contacts over the years. I mean you've got half a
million people that speak Welsh, and you soon find that it's not an awful
lot of people. It's like being in a big city. So yes, it's a very tight knit. As I
say networking within the Welsh language culture is a bit like breathing,
because, you know, it's all gossip, horribly incestuous, it drives you crazy
sometimes, but it's still quite a nice place to live.' (Morris, Translation,
Wales)

The dependence of most teleworkers on social and professional networks
for securing work had important implications for the remote working
situation. Many indicated that informal networking via the telephone, was
effective in sustaining established client contacts:

'... I just ring up lots of people and keep them informed of what I have
been doing. 'How are you? What have you been up to?' It's the discipline
every month of spending at least half a day just ringing anybody ... my
single biggest overhead is my phone bill, that probably averages about
£4500 a year ...' (Vance, Market Research, South East)

The effectiveness of such methods was greatly enhanced through personal
knowledge of established client contacts, particularly through the ability to
visualise the person at the end of the telephone. However, it was suggested
by a few respondents that, while the telephone was useful for sustaining
present client contacts, it was not adequate for establishing new clients:

'Yes, [the telephone] is fine for people I already know and I am conscious
of the fact that I can sustain very good relationships by the telephone. I am

not at all convinced that I can create new relationships ... My impression was that it would probably be very much a second, or third rate version of meeting people and I still think it is in reality. But I'm still left with this feeling that the telephone is a great way of keeping in touch with people who already know and like you and trust you, but I'm not convinced its good for creating new successful relationships, I've still got to go out and see people ...' (Matthew, Charity Consultancy, Wales)

As a result, several indicated that the most effective method of acquiring new clients was through networking with contacts via face to face interaction, at meetings, seminars and in more informal situations, such as in the corridor of an organisation:

'I try to be out 2 days a week, either with a view to having a meeting on a project or visiting clients, or just popping in, socialising with a few of them. Again cos it always leads to possibilities of business. There are some buildings you only have to walk down the corridor to get business, the fact that you're there, someone says 'oh pop in.' (Vance, Market Research, South East)

'[I get my work by] going to meetings and coming across contacts, but it's largely word of mouth. In fact you rarely meet somebody cold at a meeting and get work from it, but if you go to a meeting and there are people there that you know that maybe you've worked for, if they introduce you to somebody else and say Beth's worked for us before and so on, then that might lead to work.' (Beth, Medical Report Writer, South East)

However, working at home in the countryside did pose constraints on the levels of informal face to face networking. Although respondents stated that through necessity they visited clients to discuss work, rarely did workers have the luxury of spending time to engage in more informal and un-paid activities. Certainly, many felt that because of their location, a reduction in networking might hinder the development of their business:

'[working at home] there's no sort of, oh I bumped into so and so, I have to make an effort. I mean I belong to various trade associations and professional bodies, I rarely go to their evening meetings because, as opposed to dropping in on my way home from work, which a lot of people do, it's actually half a day's round trip for me. So I don't bother ... so I am conscious that I might miss out on that ...' (Max, Market Research, South East)

These concerns were particularly evident amongst those teleworkers in Wales who had moved into the case study areas and away from the location of their client contacts. For example, Matthew highlighted the potential implications his decision to move from London to Wales may have on the success of his business:

> 'Having moved, although I go to London, I don't see friends and contacts as much as when I was living in London, so those contacts will tend to diminish with time and I haven't yet really begun to build up local contacts, which probably won't be very local anyway, I'll probably have to go to Cardiff to find comparable work.' (Matthew, Charity Consultancy, Wales)

Despite these concerns, there was no evidence to suggest that these aspects were in any way having a negative impact on the success of respondents' businesses in terms of work flow, although clearly these factors could potentially affect the businesses over time.

While the majority of teleworkers were not dependent upon local markets for their work (arbitrarily defined as under 20 miles), several of those in the Wales case study area had experienced particular problems acquiring work within the region. These were principally associated with a lack of demand for the respondents' often specialist services. Attempts to establish markets beyond the region were constrained by the lack of client contacts in these markets and consequently, many found themselves having to overcome a weak and diverse economy by becoming less specialist, diversifying in the services they offered, and securing work from more small clients:

> 'I think one of the characteristics of this type of economy is that you have to bridge a wide range of markets, whereas if I was in London, I would be able to concentrate on one small market niche. In this kind of place, well, you've got to be able to earn your living in a wide array of markets and be damn good at it ... you're dealing basically with very small markets, so you can't survive simply on one niche market, you've got to be able to combine different ones.' (Eddie, Market Research, Wales)

> 'Well the computer graphics is one thing, working with somebody is another, and I've got plans to do something in a touristy vein. So if you look around at the locals, those that are fairly well off have inherited it, which I haven't any chance of doing, or they're doing a lot of different things, like the chap who owns the wood yard. He owns the wood yard, he's a councillor, he's got shares in a hotel, his building work, he's an undertaker. So I think doing that kind of thing is the only way of making a living. Out here I think you have to have a lot of fingers in a lot of pies.' (Phil, Graphic Design, Wales)

Businesses in the South East study area were, on the other hand, generally easier to sustain due to the concentration of demand for specialist services and the existence of more close-knit network links to clients and other businesses. Consequently, these businesses were more specialist in the services they offered.

8.5 External perceptions of teleworkers

As most of the respondents' working time was spent at home, away from clients' premises, many considered that their invisibility to clients posed potential problems for, and constraints on, their ability to secure work from organisations. Certainly, the interviews revealed that many teleworkers did perceive clients to be making particular, often negative judgements about their working situation, often influencing the way in which they actually presented, marketed and conducted themselves to organisations. For example, a few respondents in Wales expressed concern that living in a remote rural area may be perceived by clients to be unprofessional, as they were 'out on a limb':

> '... people that I deal with in London, they say, 'let me have your name and address', and I say, 'Brecon Road, Crickhowell' and they say 'where?'. If you said to somebody Cambridge, they'd know it immediately. It is out on a limb and there's no doubt about that.' (Irvin, Interior Design Consultancy, Wales)

However, the acquisition and use of ICT was being used by two teleworkers in Wales to overcome their physical remoteness and particularly the professional stigma attached to their location. For instance, Charles had moved from Bristol to Powys to set up a marketing business, but was able to disguise his rural location by using telephonic technology to divert a London telephone number to his Welsh home office and e-mail, which only provides an indication of the user's country:

> 'Certainly some people you say to, oh yes we work in Pontneathvaughan in Neath, and they say 'where?'. But with e-mail, with the right addresses and with telephones you can actually disguise where you are. And I do think it's necessary to some extent, because if I said that, it's not at the moment, but if it was a million pound company and we were based in the middle of nowhere, people like the idea of this but they need the reassurance that this is actually a big and successful company.' (Charles, Market Research, Wales)

Nevertheless, a respondent in the South East study area was actually put off from moving from just outside Brighton to a more remote rural area, as he thought his clients might make particular judgements about the nature of his working situation:

> '... and also there's other peoples' perceptions of you that are quite important. When people hear that I'm near Brighton, they can often hear the seagulls in the background when they phone me and they think, oh how wonderful that sounds while I'm in this sweat office in London, you're down there by the sea, and they all think that's wonderful, and also Brighton's got the reputation of being a slightly racey sort of place, and people take that as being OK, but if you said that you were in Great somewhere or another which sounded like it was right in the middle of nowhere, they would think that somehow you were basically semi-retired and they couldn't treat you quite as seriously as if you're a person in London, and Brighton they can think that is OK, it's not far from London and also it's an OK sort of place, but people make these judgements. I might be in an absolute hovel in Brighton they don't know that I have thought about moving to a more rural location, but living in a more rural area you feel more isolated and I think I would get less work if I was in a more rural area, but that's because of people's perceptions because people would think that I was semi-retired.' (Patrick, Journalism, South East)

Another concern expressed was that clients might feel that working at home was in some way 'unprofessional'. As a result, several respondents attempted to disguise the fact they were working at home, or tried to project a more professional image while working at home. However, due to the insecure and short-term nature of self-employment, attempts to portray a professional image often led to individuals being 'tied' to the home office:

> [The problem reassuring clients] is if you don't sound very professional - 'Sorry I didn't answer the phone I was cooking something' ... or a dog barking in the background, that can also change people's opinion about how professional they think you are. You can be perfectly professional and have a dog sitting beside you, you've got to think how it sounds to other people really ... I think you actually need to be at your desk most of the time, and if you aren't, then you leave the answerphone message which tells people how long you're going to be away from your desk for. So you come across all the time as being professional, and then people will respond well to it.' (Helen, Market Research, South East)

Other problems expressed by teleworkers related to the clients' perceptions of the individuals themselves rather than their work capability. For example, one teleworker felt that, although self-employed homeworkers can keep their age fairly disguised, prejudices may be formed when face to face contact is made with younger managers within client organisations. Despite these concerns however, only one respondent reported that judgements made by clients about their situation actually militated against the use of her services:

> 'Well I think my clients are quite comfortable with it. I got one of my quotes turned down from a company that I don't do any work for, and when I rang for feedback and I said 'Was it the price?' and she said 'no not really'. They were worried that because it was just me at home, if I became ill, then work wouldn't get finished.' (Jenny, Medical Report Writing, South East)

However, teleworkers were clear about the advantages accrued by organisations in using self-employed homeworkers rather than larger enterprises. Benefits gained included value for money, greater personal service, access to niche market skills and higher levels of personal responsibility, for example:

> 'There are lots of reasons why presumably it's worthwhile people coming to me now that I'm here rather than a big company. With a big company I haven't got that vast reputation behind me, on the other hand here, they should be able to get me all the time, so I have a car phone, a hand bag telephone ... I seem to have more time to see them. I think they see me as more accessible, more relaxed, and I would think that that means being more productive and producing higher calibre work.' (Kitty, Market Research, South East)

> 'The thing with large supplying companies, is that they've got a very smart front line staff that give presentations and appear at the first meeting, but the work is actually done by the graduate trainees and then the smart suit appears again at the presentation ... Whereas if you go to an independent, if you like the person you're talking to, the work is actually going to be done by them ... People on their own also tend to give it their all on a project ... I've got no distractions like running the company ... I don't have to go to meetings about what furniture we're going to have in the office and this sort of thing ... I mean obviously I think they get very good costs, I've got very low overheads.' (Emily, Market Research, South East)

8.6 The use of telecottages by teleworkers

While telecottages have formed the principal policy response of agencies responsible for telework facilitation in rural areas, it is far from clear how important they are within the day to day operations of successful teleworkers in the study areas, particularly in terms of providing ICT, workspace, training and marketing services for such workers.

Although about two thirds of teleworkers indicated that they were indeed aware of telecottages, only half were actually familiar with the services they offered. Awareness of telecottages was significantly higher in Wales than in the South East study area, possibly reflecting the larger number of telecottages in this area. Despite these levels of awareness and familiarity with the services offered, only five workers had ever used the services of an independent telecottage. Of these, three from the Wales study area had used the telecottage for basic IT training and the remaining two from the South East for advice on teleworking and access to photocopying and scanning. None had used the telecottage as a workspace nor been supplied with work or had their skills marketed by such an enterprise. All of the teleworkers that had used the telecottage were operating routine businesses such as business/secretarial services, and it was apparent that they had contacted telecottages in order to help them develop their teleworking business, albeit with little success, for example:

'I went on a teleworking course at SIMTRA [telecottage], and to be honest it was very very basic. I was hoping to learn about modems and ISDN lines, and the amount it told me was very basic and it wasn't really very helpful. I knew as much when I went there as when I came away. We wanted to learn about costing and how you went about finding work, looking for contracts, how you did all this, but it didn't touch on those. So I was a bit disillusioned. It didn't set you up to go on to teleworking at all.'
(Sonia, Secretarial/Business Services, Wales)

The limited demand for telecottages as a central ICT resource can be linked to the indication by the majority of teleworkers that they had all the equipment they needed and preferred to invest in any extra equipment they required. A key factor of these responses was the reducing costs of technology and the convenience of having the equipment, such as faxes and computers, in their own homes. Several respondents did suggest that a central ICT resource might be useful for those starting up in business but not wanting to invest in the equipment. Others, however, argued that as the cost of the technology was so small, those with a definite intention of starting a business would tend to acquire the equipment independently.

These findings therefore question the whole idea of the telecottage as a central ICT resource, particularly in supporting or facilitating telework, as one teleworker suggested:

> 'Some people's argument for telecottages was that people couldn't afford the technology, to buy a computer, to buy a fax. Well I'm very suspicious of that argument. You could equally say, well, people can't afford to buy a car. I'm convinced that if people really need it, they will make the investment, because the investment in relative terms isn't that great by now is it, lets face facts. You could get pretty far on 1500 quid. Now how far would you get on 1500 quid if you wanted to buy a car? So what seems to me to be the case is that this technology really is very, very cheap. In what other field could you envisage a situation where you could buy a pretty vital means of earning a living for 1500 pounds? It doesn't exist. If you wanted to establish yourself as a carpenter, and wanted to buy the equipment, you'd spend a damn sight more than 1500 quid.' (Eddie, Market Research, Wales)

As for the use of telecottages as communal workspaces, a few people recognised the potential advantages working in such an environment might bring, including greater social interaction and the ability to separate home and work. However, no teleworkers had used a telecottage for these purposes and there generally appeared to be no intention of using one for such at a later date. Furthermore, the majority of respondents indicated certain negative aspects associated with working in a communal workspace, particularly in contrast to working at home:

> 'It has all the disadvantages of working in an office, and none of the advantages of working from home. I mean why sacrifice all the advantages, which is, no commuting, and being with your family and being able to nip in and out ... I would never consider it. I mean I've got a house, I've got a room in a house, what's the point of renting another?' (Edmund, Translation, Wales)

Many teleworkers expressed other distinct disadvantages of working in a telecottage, such as incurring unnecessary overheads and the inevitability of interruptions, which, as chapter seven highlighted, several respondents had tried to escape by becoming self-employed teleworkers.

As for acquiring training from a telecottage, several respondents suggested that potential and actual teleworkers generally tended to be technologically proficient and as such would not require ICT training, typically provided by telecottages. Moreover, although a few teleworkers did indicate that future career development was restricted and dependent upon attending private, and often expensive, courses and seminars, they did not consider telecottages to have the expertise or reputation to deliver such training sessions. Furthermore, as contacts in the industry were successfully used by most teleworkers to secure work, telecottages were considered to play only a very limited role in marketing and securing work for teleworkers.

8.7 Summary

This chapter has focused on the characteristics and dynamics of telework in the study areas, particularly in relation to the location of clients and methods of communicating and securing work. In terms of the general characteristics of the teleworking businesses, it was clearly apparent that differences within the case study areas were often as significant as differences between them. Indeed, distance from markets and levels of remote and direct interaction with clients was determined as much by the residential dynamics of, and the types of services traded by, teleworkers, as by their geographical location.

Whilst there was evidence indicating significant interregional and international exchange of work, there remained a regional orientation in the clients served by certain teleworkers. This reflected the concentration of clients in the same area as teleworkers' previous employer[s] and subsequently the fact that most workers had not relocated since becoming self-employed. Teleworkers with the most remote clients tended to be those who had moved into the case study areas from predominantly urban centres where their client contacts were located. Teleworking translators also exhibited considerable flexibility in terms of the location of markets due to structuring of the translation market around the use of international teleworkers.

Teleworkers demonstrated a heavy reliance on ICT as well as more traditional forms of remote communications to undertake work, although use of more advanced telecommunications technologies, such as modems, were constrained by the limited adoption of, and familiarity with, such technologies amongst client organisations. However, certain respondents, particularly those involved in consultancy and market research, still found it necessary to meet their clients on a face to face basis regardless of the location of clients and the costs involved. Teleworking translators and journalists on the other hand, required less direct interaction as tasks undertaken did not require as much input from clients.

Direct face to face interaction was, however, considered important for the development of new clients, as ICT and more traditional marketing methods were ineffective in this respect. While certain respondents, particularly in Wales, who worked for remote markets, were concerned as to how, because of their location, a reduction in networking opportunities may affect work flow, there was no evidence to suggest that it was currently having a negative effect on the business.

While the majority of businesses were successful in terms of income and work flow, the concentrations of industry and commerce in the South East of England meant that businesses tended to be more specialised and were generally easier to establish and sustain. On the other hand, those businesses in the Wales study area serving predominantly regional markets had to be more adaptable and diverse in the markets they served.

Several respondents were conscious of how they were perceived by clients and, through various means, attempted to portray a more professional image, whether through disguising their location or through carefully managing their home-office environment. Respondents were also aware of the many cost and non-cost advantages they offered organisations. In terms of the use of telecottages by teleworkers, it was clear that the actual and future demand for telecottage services was negligible. This related primarily to the reducing costs of technology, low levels of social isolation experienced by respondents, their familiarity with ICT and the existence of markets based upon personal experience and contacts.

This Chapter has highlighted the dynamics and characteristics of telework within the two case study areas. The final survey chapter shifts the focus on to the wider experiences of teleworking in the countryside.

9 The Wider Experience of Teleworking

9.1 Introduction

Chapter Seven highlighted key factors and motivations underpinning the decision to telework in the study areas. However, it was argued earlier that such motivating factors are not necessarily the same ones which retain the worker in that situation and the extent to which people will continue to telework will depend on the experiences of that situation and their changing social and economic circumstances. This final survey chapter explores the problems and advantages of self-employed teleworking in the two study areas.

9.2 The experience of self-employment

9.2.1 Autonomy and control

Self-employment more generally has been associated with particular individualistic attitudes termed the 'philosophy of self-employment', emphasising flexibility, autonomy, choice and freedom in the work process (Leighton, 1982). Certainly, the advantages of 'being one's own boss' were expressed universally amongst the respondents with benefits typically stated in relation to the previous negative experiences of working within an organisation. For example:

> 'It's also quite nice to be a freelancer, quite nice to know that you're making it on your own, or through your own efforts. So you're not sort of being carried along by the equivalent of a truck, a giant truck, do you know what I mean? You're not being sort of supported by some flabby organisation that drags you along with it. There's a slightly nomadic feeling about it.' (Edmund, Translation, Wales)

Although this quotation suggests that feelings of autonomy were predominantly psychological, there was considerable evidence to suggest that feelings were based on real freedoms and flexibilities of self-employed telework. Typically such freedoms related to being able to control work flows, work tasks, leisure time and client sectors served:

> '[The advantages are] flexibility in terms of being able to take time off when you want, and on the other hand being able to work on, late at night, and being able to work for different organisations.' (Muriel, Translation, Wales)

> 'Being your own boss, you get treated with a lot more respect as a freelance operator than you do if you're a cog in a big institute. Somebody phones you up and you have too much work, you can say 'sorry, I can't take on any more work', but if you're in a company ... someone says 'I want you to do this'. You know you don't have to put up with all that hassle.' (Jane, Translation, South East)

> 'As you know we've had a marvellous summer, and therefore I have deliberately cut down the work load that I would have in the summer. Come September and right through the winter I'll be working six to seven days a week. So on balance I still work more than I want, and intended, but I have the choice to do that. Being in the situation of working from home does facilitate that.' (Brendan, Training Consultancy, Wales)

Nevertheless, although teleworkers expressed that their work was flexible, most indicated working relatively long hours. While several respondents, mainly mothers, tried to keep to under a 40 hour week, the majority worked in excess of this:

> 'In a typical working week I would say I am actually working here four days and two days out. It's a six day week minimum throughout, and I would say inter dispersed with seven day weeks every fourth or fifth week ...You do get some extremes. If I'm doing a 70 hour week I feel as though I'm redundant, I'm serious, absolutely serious.' (Vance, Market Research, South East)

Such intense working patterns were particularly common amongst those workers with high turnovers, typically involved in providing specialist services such as consultancy and market research. However, the stresses of long hours were often compensated by the perception that work input was directly proportional to revenue, unlike within conventional employment:

> '[The advantages are] control of your own destiny really, that's it. You can work as hard or as little as you want to, and in many ways the remuneration and reward are almost in direct proportion. Whereas you can go and work for someone else, you can work your backside off, and the

rewards are certainly not in the same proportion in any way.' (Phillip, Interior Design Consultancy, Wales)

Certain commentators have argued that within some forms of self-employment there exists an illusion of autonomy and control which is tightly grasped as it helps to compensate for the realities of working long hours, being even more tied to work and being dependent on bank managers as opposed to employers (Hakim, 1988). Indeed, several respondents mentioned that, whilst in theory control over their work did exist, the realities of running a small business meant that such freedoms were rarely appropriated to their fullest extent. Nonetheless, it was apparent that, because they had the feeling of control and that work was self-imposed, it was less of a concern to them:

'I am much more, in theory, I have much more control over my life. In theory I have a lot more say over what I do and don't do. In practice I have none. I suppose it doesn't matter because it makes me feel a lot better about it, the fact that I am stupidly busy is my own fault and the fact that I am running around like a maniac. At least I can console myself, well at least I'm making some money out of it, and there's a direct correlation between my work input and my out-take.' (Max, Market Research, South East)

9.2.2 Insecurity

Other experiences, however, did reflect particular problems associated with self-employment. While there existed dominant feelings of autonomy and independence amongst respondents, a common concern related to the short-term nature of self-employment and more specifically contract work. Feelings of insecurity were expressed by over two thirds of respondents, including those 'workstyle' and 'lifestyle' respondents, identified in chapter seven, who tended to be the most optimistic and positive entrants to self-employment:

'Well there are problems in that I can be reasonably confident that I'm still in work for the next four months, but after that, it's all very uncertain and that's inherent to my situation. But if I'm not able to finish a contract within four months, then the client won't be interested, so it's an act of faith that somebody out there will be requiring my services four months down the line. Now, that's pressure, that's uncertainty, but you've got to live with it, and I think a lot of people are living with that kind of pressure.' (Brendan, Training Consultancy, Wales)

'It's bad for your nerves, in that you're never quite sure whether you're going to have the income. Although our commitments aren't very high, you sort of get this feeling of living a bit hand to mouth if you like. I mean I am earning a reasonable amount of money, but you're not sure how long it's going to go on for ...' (Catherine, Journalism, South East)

Indeed, many of the stresses and pressures attributed to self-employment by respondents appeared to be rooted in the psychological difficulties of controlling and predicting work flow. More specifically, teleworkers feared that, although they may be overloaded with work, they did not want to turn away clients with work which may not be there in the future. These experiences were particularly evident in the initial stages of the business when relationships with clients were at their weakest:

'... most people find it difficult to say no [to work], because you always think that if I say no to this, there might not be anymore next week, because you can't plan more than a few weeks ahead.' (Jane, Translation, South East)

'At the beginning, in the first year or two, ... I'd be trying to do everything that the customer asked of me, you're building up your contacts, trying to establish links, trying to please everybody ...' (Ivor, Translation, Wales)

Nevertheless, it was apparent that these feelings of insecurity did not necessarily equate with the reality of the working situation, as the majority of teleworkers stated that they had never had longer than a day without work. Only three workers had significant periods without work and they were providing non-specialist routine functions such as business/secretarial services and who, as has been stated, experienced problems in establishing markets for their routine services.

Around a third of respondents considered their clients and contracts secure, which, although often short-term, for example from a day to several months, were regular. Within this group of teleworkers, high levels of familiarity and informality had developed with clients from previous employment, but also from the acquisition and renewal of contracts over time. Familiarity with clients was accompanied by a set of distinct advantages relating to the general ability to control the working situation:

'It depends how well your clients know you. If they know you, and want you, then you don't feel beholden to jump. That's the advantage of a long term client relationship. If it's a short term thing, like say I was a graphic designer or something where you have to respond immediately, then of course it's not nearly so easy.' (Neil, Computer Consultancy, South East)

Other advantages related to the ability to approach clients for work rather than reacting to offers of work; being able to turn work down without the fear of clients not returning; and, in a few cases, receiving preferential treatment in terms of receiving contracts over other workers.

While most respondents aspired to more secure client relationships, several, most of whom were located in the South East study area, expressed a desire to become less dependent on clients. Amongst this group, serving small numbers of very regular clients engendered feelings of insecurity and a fear of over-reliance:

> '... there are a few key clients which is nice but it's a bit dangerous ... but it means that your eggs are in a small number of baskets. [They have lasted] so far, 18 months to three years, but you never know when their next axe is going to fall really.' (Laura, European Business Consultancy, South East)

Fears of having 'your eggs in a small number of baskets' often led to attempts to diversify and establish a broader client base:

> '[I want] to diversify so I don't get a sort of ridiculous amount of my work from one organisation, so that if they decided that they don't like me, or the publication is shelved or something, and I'm not suddenly looking round for a huge percentage of my income ...' (Patrick, Journalism, South East)

Inevitably, however, respondents encountered the dilemma of trying to generate new contracts and relationships when established clients kept offering work:

> 'I've had two phone calls in the last week asking me to do work, and although I realise it could leave me exposed if they decide to pull out, it seems crazy to turn down the work at the moment ... and I'm certainly building enough of the cash reserves that if they do pull out, I can generate some sort of salary for myself while I go round looking for other clients.' (Jenny, Medical Report Writing, South East)

9.3 The experience of homeworking

9.3.1 Integration of home and workspace

It has been suggested that working at home has many advantages, particularly for those restricted to, or wishing to, work at home (Huws et al,

1990, Stanworth and Stanworth, 1991). Certainly, it was revealed earlier that a number of female respondents in the study area were attracted to self-employed telework due to the flexibilities of working for oneself at home and being able to integrate childcare and professional employment. However, the interviews also revealed that virtually all of the mothers indicated that they did not attempt to work while their children were at home. While respondents in Wales tended to work when their children were at nursery, with a childminder, or in bed, those in the South East, who generally had greater household incomes, employed childminders, au pairs and nannies to enable them to work full-time. Therefore it was evident that self-employed teleworking did not totally eliminate the need for childcare, but enabled mothers to cope with the temporal and spatial demands and uncertainties of being a mother:

'[I have flexibility] in terms of time and also in terms of the children. I mean, if my son comes home and says I'm reading in assembly, or our class is doing assembly, that usually means a Friday morning's first hour is taken up by going to that. Well I can do that because I don't have a boss to say you can't have the time off, and I can just adjust my work load slightly, work a bit harder, take my dog for a shorter walk and enjoy that assembly.' (Jenny, Translation, South East)

'The real positive things are it has allowed me a lot of flexibility with the children, because if ever they were off school sick, you can just instantly juggle things around a bit to be at home, and that really was the main priority.' (Evelyn, Journalism, South East)

It emerged earlier that for nearly three quarters of respondents, the decision to work at home was not a major factor in opting to become a self-employed teleworker, instead relating to the conveniences and cost benefits of homeworking. Nonetheless, clear advantages of homeworking, such as cost; reduced interruptions; flexibility to cope with family activities; the reduction in commuting; and increased productivity were given by teleworkers, illustrated by the following response:

'... every minute of the day from nine to five is productive time, and not spending three hours a day travelling like I used to do. Very low overheads, working from home. In a way that has a positive effect on the prices that you are able to quote to people, which can be an influence on why you get business.' (Evelyn, Journalism, South East)

The narrowing of the gap between professional and home life through telework can also create a set of potential conflicts within the home.

Indeed, most respondents, including the more positive and optimistic 'workstyle' and 'lifestyle' respondents, experienced a set of problems relating to the integration of home and workspace:

'The advantages are that there's no travelling to work. On the other hand, there's no travelling from work, in the sense that your work is always a couple of yards away from you.' (Eddie, Market Research, Wales)

This aspect was manifest in the inability of teleworkers to differentiate work and home, both temporally and spatially. This inability to switch off from work because of the psychological and spatial proximity between work and home was a common problem:

'... there is no cut off ... if I was at home, and I finished my work in the office, there wouldn't be anything else to do. I'd be here, and what else would I do, but because there's always work here, it's quite difficult to pull yourself away from anything.' (Gill, Journalism, South East)

Although not a universal concern, the following respondent expressed particular problems of how the responsibilities of being self-employed were compounded by operating the business in the home. Dominant feelings of the home as a place of work, engendered desires to escape that space, often conflicting with other family wishes:

'... various times when I have been working at home, I had felt almost that I didn't want to come into the house sometimes, because as soon as you come in, there are problems here, and normally your house, your home, is one place where you can shut your work problems out. But when they're actually in the house, sometimes when you come to the front door, you can really feel a sense of dread, what's going to be in there, what's on the answerphone whatever? And also I think your family like to spend time at home at weekends, and you find that when you are at home all the time you actually want to go out and get out at the weekends which is in conflict with the family and what they want to do.' (Evelyn, Journalism, South East)

In more practical terms, however, having a home office meant that respondents were always 'available' to clients. As a result, the psychological problems of work being 'a couple of yards away from you' were intensified by permanent interruptions from phone calls:

'... if you're working from home, then OK you're at home but you're working, but your work invades your home life as well. The commonest time for people to ring me is between five and six which is the worst time when you're at home because the children are at home and you're trying to get their dinner. But that's the commonest time for people to ring, because they're just coming to the end of their working day, so they make phone calls in the evening.' (Matthew, Charity Consultancy, Wales)

'[The problems with working at home are] because it's here, not being able to actually stop and because the telephone line is the same. Not being able to get away from people ringing you up about work ... although you can say, 'look I'm not working today', or 'I'm not doing it', I am very bad at that and I think that's the main [problem], the fact that it's here. But on the other hand I wouldn't really want an office in town because then I'd have to go to it, and it would be a drag. I couldn't work at 11 or 12 o'clock at night.' (Eve, Market Research, Wales)

Other teleworkers experienced additional problems connected to their workspace. For example, one respondent had a corner of the landing in which to work and complained of being interrupted every time someone came up the stairs. Another lived and worked on a converted fishing boat in a South coast marina and experienced problems of having to put work away every time she and her partner wanted to eat, and of being reliant upon an on-board generator to power her computer, which often failed to work on cold mornings.

It emerged from the interviews with teleworkers that the psychological and practical difficulties of homeworking were less of a concern for the several respondents who had workspaces separate from the immediate homespace, such as in converted garages or log cabins in the garden. In these cases the physical separation of workspace and living space was considered essential to enable them to separate their home and work life:

'[A separate workspace] ... was very important to me and I looked for a house that did have this kind of facility. It was important because I didn't want my work to be part of whatever was going on in the house. But I also wanted it to be separate, so if the kids are having a fight or wanted to play music, I didn't have to worry about being on the phone. I did think before I worked at home, that I would not feel professional, and I also thought it was important to be dressed to go to work, but I find it doesn't matter at all that I can sit here in jeans and I can produce the same quality of work as if I am sitting here in a suit. Having a separate office helps. I am a particular type of person here but then I have a different personality when I am in there. What also is important is that I have two phones, one for business and one for private.' (Laura, European Business Consultancy, South East)

'... I'm very lucky here, because to get to my office you go out that door and up another set of stairs and although I've got the office phone there, when I'm here I can't hear the office phone and when I'm in the office I can't hear the house phone. So because of this particular building, I have created a physical barrier between work and home, and so work time and leisure time are physically separated even though the day should be blurred ... I would feel that it would be more of a problem if work was a corner of the living room, or work was the next door along the corridor or whatever, rather than being a separate place. I suppose it would be different if the work wasn't of my own creation, if it was somebody else's work I was doing ...' (Max, Market Research, South East)

Therefore, while such respondents achieved all of the benefits of living and working at home, they did not suffer the practical and psychological difficulties expressed by others working in the home.

9.3.2 Professional and social isolation

Although it has been claimed that social isolation is a considerable problem facing home-based teleworkers (Huws et al, 1990), social isolation was only mentioned by a few respondents as a significant problem. All of these were female workers in the South East study area, who had previously held 'professional' positions within large organisations and appeared to be more sensitive to the social implications of being withdrawn from office environments:

'I think I realise I need people. I do need people and it's probably why I enjoyed being in a job, and that's why I realised I'm not really cut out to work on my own, I'm not very good at it ...' (Jessica, Recruitment Consultancy, South East)

'I think there's only one problem and that's that you don't get enough contact with people, well you can if you work at it, but you have to work at it. It doesn't come naturally ... just the human contact, working with a team with other people, being part of the organisation, you have to consciously find a substitute for that.' (Gill, Journalism, South East)

Certainly, the fact that social isolation was not expressed as a major concern by most respondents raises the question of whether they were immune to it or whether levels of isolation were being reduced by some other means. Chapter Eight demonstrated that most respondents had close knit networks of former colleagues and client contacts. It also emerged from the interviews that most respondents had developed local and more distant networks of other small businesses via organisations such as the Chamber of Commerce, professional bodies and local business groups. It was these networks, sustained through extensive and regular verbal interaction via the telephone and occasional face to face meetings, helped reduce feelings of isolation:

'Do I feel isolated? No because the phone is ringing all day. The people I talk to on the phone I know by sight anyway.' (Morris, Translation, Wales)

'But in terms of loneliness, or things like that, well I'm never, well almost never lonely, because there's always people like Sarah phoning up who wants to talk for half an hour and other freelancers will phone me. And then a lot of my time is spent on the phone to get material for features, so I don't feel I have to see the people. If nobody ever phoned that would make you lonely but basically the phone rings all the time ...' (Patrick, Journalism, South East)

'I've got a network of freelance colleagues that are working all over the place. There's one good friend who we work on projects together and I see him more than most mainly through work. If I get bored or fed up, I'll call up any one of a number of colleagues.' (Mark, Journalism, South East)

Certainly, the female respondents, who had experienced isolation, suggested that many of the associated problems were overcome by joining professional groups and local business clubs such as Women in Business and the Chamber of Commerce where they could meet like-minded individuals:

'I tried [to remedy social isolation] through groups like WIB [Women in Business], and the Enterprise Agency and the Business Club. I think it's really quite important that you have contact with people working in a similar situation, because it's lovely talking to people who have got the same difficulties or problems, and very often I ring up a friend about something awful that's happened or that I just want to talk to somebody and you catch them on a really good day and then they'll be ringing you up maybe a few weeks later and you're actually feeling really positive about everything, and when they're down, you reciprocate. I used to meet up with friends every third Friday morning in the month for coffee in East Grinstead and have a chat about things, and obviously a lot of networking goes on tremendously between people that are self-employed.' (Evelyn, Journalism, South East)

'[working at home] there are losses in that you don't have anyone else around you in the office, so you've got to fix things up to make sure you don't get isolated. Because in a business sense you can get very isolated from ideas, you've got to keep in contact with people. The things that I do, I go to Women in Business. It doesn't give me any business ideas but it just makes me feel part of the business community. I belong to the chamber of commerce you can belong to your own professional organisations, I don't belong to the NUJ but you could. But you're really got to join up with some of these things otherwise you are working in a complete vacuum really.' (Gill, Journalism, South East)

Professional isolation, on the other hand, was expressed as a significant problem by almost all of the respondents. These concerns related primarily to the lack of professional stimulation and interaction normally available in conventional office environments. For example:

'I've never had it really, the ability to bounce ideas off of somebody else, and this is a common problem. And I was speaking to someone who works in the same situation as I do, and she was saying to me yesterday, that it was driving her around the bend not being able to communicate and bounce ideas off people. I had a French student working with me for two months in the summer, and that was great to work with someone who was committed and interested and involved and she would offer ideas and you realise that you may be going down one route and not even realise that there are little sort of side roads you should be going down ...' (Laura, European Business Consultancy, South East)

Recruitment from external labour markets also meant that self-employed teleworkers were often not involved on a long-term basis with organisations. As such, a few respondents expressed problems about not receiving feedback on their work and not having the long-term continuity of one organisation and seeing it develop.

Another key problem was the lack of personal and career development opportunities for teleworkers. As most respondents had developed their expertise within an organisation, chances to develop other areas of expertise were very restricted. Whilst several suggested that specialist training courses did help them diversify into other areas of work, they considered that ultimately clients would only contract workers to take on tasks they knew they were capable of undertaking:

'I cannot see how you develop your career. People will phone me up and give me lots of work doing what I do, but nobody is going to phone me up and give me a chance to do something different.' (Max, Market Research, South East)

9.4 The experience of living and working in the countryside

It was highlighted in Chapter Seven that for over a third of respondents, becoming self-employed was either preceded or followed by relocation into the case study areas. Perhaps unsurprisingly, it was amongst this group that the advantages of living and working in the countryside were most clearly expressed. Typically advantages related to a better physical environmental, improved social relations and to the general advantages of being remote from particular (and in some cases previously experienced) city lifestyles:

> 'I can grow my own vegetables, can look out over nice landscapes which are not laced with pylons and petrol station signs and things. Human relations here are pretty good as a whole, people are quite relaxed because people are not pressed together and they don't infringe each others private space, and people aren't all that paranoid as other people are in other places. The air is clean, children can play outside, climb trees, go swimming, things like that they can't do in cities. I mean I lived in Japan ... I knew of people that lived in blocks of flats in the city, and the children didn't really do anything, I mean they played video games and they watched TV and they read comics, and that's how their childhood was spent. Horrifying really.' (Edmund, Translation, Wales)

Certainly for many of these teleworkers, such employment and residential transitions represented complete lifestyle and workstyle shifts, from being an employee, living and working in or near a city, to being self-employed in the countryside. Indeed, it was highlighted earlier that representations of telework have often been rooted in particular notions of complete life and workstyle shifts. While it appears that such representations have been based on perhaps idyllic notions of telework, the experiences of these individuals tended to emphasise the reality of the satisfactions achieved by engaging in such changes:

> 'Oh it's absolutely brilliant, completely different way of life, I mean, cut the stress right out because it was fairly stressful, certainly within the telecoms market. Office politics were quite stressful, it got to the point where, I don't actually need this. This way of life is very, very nice, I mean it's been a stunning summer which has really not helped in a way, cos it gets so hot in here that you end up, getting to about three o'clock and wanting to bunk off to the river for a swim or something.' (Charles, Market Research, Wales)

> 'We lived in Battersea where the streets were very busy, very heavy with parked cars and security was bad. So when I got back from the office, I

had to bring out of the car my telephone, my radio, pick up a child, and some shopping and a brief case, and quite often I had to park three streets away, and I never knew whether to leave the child in the car, and think they'd nick the car, or the child in the house. So it was the pressures really of living in very crowded streets that really brought it about ... Well this is a wonderful office to work in because I can look out in the garden, I can see the children playing without being distracted by it, particularly in the good weather. One has all the fun of being in a pretty place ... I've had a client party here which was madly successful in the summer it was wonderful, but I think, I don't know, it's just, although I can't switch off as easy as I could when I was working for someone else, I'm still in a nice place thinking about work rather than in an awful place thinking about work. And I haven't got to sit in jams and get frustrated about not doing anything.' (Kitty, Market Research, South East)

A decrease in the levels of interaction with work colleagues through teleworking has been linked with a possible increase in the levels of community interaction and participation at the local level (Toffler, 1980, Blanc, 1988). While it was difficult to establish whether there was an inverse relationship between these two levels of interaction, several respondents indicated that working at home did enable them to take a more active part in their community, as illustrated by the following responses:

'[We're very involved in village life] because I'm here and she's here and we make an effort. It's very easy not to make an effort, to wrap yourself up in your own little world ... We intend to be here for a long time, and a lot of people commute, but their job changes and they'll be off.' (Neil, Computer Consultancy, South East)

'I'm on the committee of the local horticultural society, and they had a meeting on Monday, which I was able to go to because I work from home.. I went to the post office on the way, and had a chat to the person in the village shop and got some bits to have for lunch. I called in at the woman who's the Parish Council Secretary to do some photocopying ... So I've seen a lot of people just today ...' (Max, Market Research, South East)

'I mean, if I was at work all day, I wouldn't see anyone hardly at all. I would just be an absentee person, the house would be dark and we just wouldn't be here, I think that would be sad.' (Eve, Market Research, Wales)

However, greater interaction with neighbours and people in the local community did, for several respondents, appear to be problematic for their work, particularly when neighbours, assuming that because respondents were at home they were not working, felt they could pop round for a chat as, and when, they wanted.

9.5 Future plans and aspirations

9.5.1 Job satisfaction and future employment plans

Despite certain negative factors associated with self-employed telework, the majority of respondents did not consider that such factors inhibited their working situation. Indeed, particular remedies, such as building client relationships, separating work and homespace and integrating into networks of other small businesses, have appeared to reduce the negative aspects of self-employed telework. Ultimately, virtually all respondents stated that, although their situation was not problem-free, it was far superior to the alternative opportunities available within conventional employment, and did not consider going back to an employee job. These opinions were also evident amongst those 'childcare', 'unemployed in-migrants' 'threat of unemployment' and 'forced unemployment' teleworkers, discussed in Chapter Seven, who generally chose self-employment in part because of the lack of alternative employment opportunities. For example:

'For me to go back into a company, I've said all along, I would literally have to go without a day's work for six months, and you know, a real prospect that there's never going to be another day's work for whatever reason, for me to even entertain any kind of full-time employment again with an employer.' (Phillip, Interior Design Consultancy, Wales)

'I would never want to go back to working for a large organisation ever. I visit quite a lot of large organisations as clients, and I just look in horror at the whole set up. Upstairs I have a very nice quiet office where nobody disturbs me at all, I can lay myself out all over the room if I want to, nobody is going to disturb me. I can work the hours I want to work, I mean I have one child at home now, and if I'm working at home, I do pick her up from school ... She goes to bed at seven, I go back to work. That's my concern and it's nothing to do with anybody else.' (Emily, Market Research, South East)

Certainly, while several respondents were aware of the attractions of security within conventional employment, a similar number perceived insecurity to be inherent within conventional employment anyway:

'It's less stability and security, but I think that's a chimera anyway these days. I don't believe people have a job for life, there's no way, ... I mean the pressure on industry and commerce is so high, and the idea that people have a job for life is gone. People have a duty, a responsibility to themselves and to their own futures ...' (Linda, Training Consultancy, South East)

Only three teleworkers expressed an intention to re-enter conventional employment and, even here, there was no plan of leaving self-employment completely. For example, one respondent in Wales found that demand for his specialised graphic design and slide production business was declining, particularly amongst the local client base. As such he was considering taking a part-time job to supplement his income. For the other two workers, problems of homeworking, and more specifically feelings of isolation engendered by working out of an organisational environment, prompted them to look for an additional job outside of the home. For example:

'... it was really at that point where I thought well perhaps I should try and do something part-time out of the house, that will get me back with other professional people.' (Evelyn, Journalism, South East)

9.5.2 Residential plans

It was demonstrated in Chapter Seven that for a quarter of respondents, the decision to telework was either accompanied or superseded by a residential shift. However, twice this number of other teleworkers were clearly aware of the potential residential mobility of their working situation. Indeed, several indicated definite plans for future re-location:

'[I'd like to move to] somewhere very rural. A lot of translators are now moving out, to the Hebrides, Shetland, Mid Wales, Lake District. I would go either Dorset way or maybe Scotland or somewhere like that. Well the job's changed, when I started 12 years ago people weren't using all the electronic things they are now. I mean now as long as you've got a phone line and electricity you can be anywhere. You need a fax, a modem and a phone line.' (Jane, Translation, South East)

Others, however, had more adventurous plans; for example, one teleworker was planning to move his work and his life onto a canal boat. Another, already living and working on a boat, indicated that by acquiring more advanced technology, she could take her boat and her work to the South of France, as she already had done successfully on a previous occasion:

'Well with satellite communications there's no reason why I can't move from here. All the technologies are getting cheaper so there's absolutely no reason why I can't be in the South of France getting a document down line and working on it that day, and in fact when we were in the South of France I worked on a couple of training workbooks, so it's totally feasible.' (Linda, Training Consultancy, South East)

Thus, while only a quarter of teleworkers interviewed had appropriated the locational flexibilities of telework, the considerable awareness of this potential amongst the remaining respondents meant that realisation of residential preferences over time could increase this number.

9.5.3 Growth and expansion

While it was highlighted in earlier sections that all respondents intended staying in self-employment, it emerged from the interviews that they had no aspirations to expand the business. Many of the factors such as autonomy and control, which led them to set up on their own, were the same factors that motivated them to keep the business small:

'I took a decision fairly early on in freelance that I didn't want to employ anyone else. I did not want to be an employer, and as far as possible I wanted to be a sole trading, a sort of artisan, someone who has their own tools, and works on particular things and goes form job to job. But that's a personal decision, I've never had any aspirations to run a company, I don't want to be a company I don't want that whole culture.' (Matthew, Charity Consultancy, Wales)

It was also evident that such aspirations did not change with the realisation of the growth potential of the business. For example, in a few cases, forces for expansion were strongly resisted:

'I have fought very hard to stop my business growing actually, against all the feeling that businesses should be encouraged to grow and all the rest of it, I don't want it to, because I want it to stay manageable for me, and ... you know, other people will come in probably at a higher level and do that stuff, but I don't really want to. It's the sort of sustainable bit of it really.' (Eve, Market Research, Wales)

'I have been asked several times, 'Could I expand? Could I take on staff?' The answer's yes I could have done on several occasions. I could have taken on premises, I could have taken on all sorts of overheads. I have been advised by everybody I know that owns a small business, if you can manage it on your own stay on your own, cos apparently the minute you take on staff, the minute you take on premises, you end up not doing what you love, you end up becoming a manager of people, and an administrator.' (Vance, Market Research, South East)

Despite this evidence, several teleworkers had been involved in indirect expansion through collaboration on contracts with other self-employed professionals and through the use of other local self-employed individuals to undertake administrative and secretarial tasks. Indeed, a few of those respondents who were providing routine secretarial and business services indicated individual professional teleworkers amongst their clients. This kind of collaboration had an important role to play in reducing the negative effects of professional isolation, highlighted earlier:

'One of [the problems] is myopia which is you never ever have anybody else giving you a different opinion, different point of view, you don't have anybody to bounce ideas off. I sometimes worry that I always approach problems in the same way because that's the only way that comes naturally to me. And that's one of the reasons why I like to work with other people if I can.' (Max, Market Research, South East)

One respondent, however, highlighted the difficulties of using external teleworking sub-contractors. Although the ability to telework meant that the location of potential workers was not of concern, the importance of personal expertise and experience on the teleworking business was considered a constraint to expansion:

'I am beginning to wonder whether I should have some sort of back up system, you know, find somebody around here, or anywhere. I mean I'm on the Internet, so they could be in Mexico for all I care, who can actually take over if there's too much. But the problem is, it's not that I'm a perfectionist particularly, but I do like to get everything perfect. The fact is I would still have to read their work to make sure everything is all right.' (Edmund, Translation, Wales)

It was apparent therefore, that, while many of these businesses did not want to expand beyond what they considered to be an optimal and efficient size for their operation, several had developed networks of sub-contractors enabling mutual expansion without the bureaucratic and economic implications of more conventional methods of expansion.

9.6 Summary

In terms of the general experience of self-employed telework, there were no significant differences between the two case study areas. Rather there existed a common set of issues which were of concern to all those undertaking these working practices. As for self-employment, dominant feelings of autonomy, control and flexibility were accompanied by feelings of insecurity engendered by the short-term nature of sub-contracting, although these latter feelings were predominantly psychological. The long hours and stresses of self-employment were often compensated by feelings of control over the situation and that work effort was directly proportional to revenue.

In terms of homeworking, while most respondents had a dedicated office in their house, a number found it necessary to create a workspace at home as opposed to in their home, because of certain psychological and practical problems associated with working in the immediate homespace. Levels of social isolation appeared to be relatively low due to extensive interaction with clients, ex-colleagues and networks of other small businesses via the telephone and occasional face to face contact. Professional isolation was, on the other hand, expressed as a major problem, although several teleworkers had begun to co-operate with other small businesses in undertaking contracts which helped reduce these feelings.

It was those respondents who had moved to the countryside, either to establish or after establishing the business, who most clearly expressed the advantages of a rural lifestyle. Such changes often involved complete workstyle and lifestyle shifts from being an employee, living and working in the city, to being a self-employed homeworker in the countryside. In addition, while several respondents had already appropriated the spatial flexibility of telework to re-locate into the study areas, many more were aware of such opportunities and had indicated potential residential shifts to more remote rural locations and to more flexible residences such as a boat.

Although most respondents were very satisfied with their situation, expressing no intention of shifting out of self-employment, none intended to expand the business in respect of employment and premises due to the perceived attractions of keeping the business small. However, as indicated above, a number of teleworkers had been involved in a form of expansion, through collaboration with other self-employed teleworkers.

The following final chapter will bring together the findings from the last six chapters to form a comprehensive summary and conclusion.

10 Summary and Conclusion

10.1 Introduction

Telework has been linked with a de-urbanisation of employment and a shift to hi-tech homeworking in the countryside, engendering notions of telework as a panacea for many of society's ills. However, while the hype and speculation have been overwhelming, research into rural telework has been piecemeal, fragmented and often policy orientated. Research into telework generally has been more rigorous, but it has also been largely atheoretical and neglected particular geographical aspects of telework. The research presented in this book has been original and distinctive, both in its focus on telework in a specific geographical context and in relation to its in-depth approach to the subject. This final chapter brings together some of the key findings and relates them to wider debates on telework and the rural economy.

10.2 The nature of telework in rural Britain

Although telework has often been linked to the exploitation of a marginal, low skilled and low paid workforce, the demand for self-employed telework has been primarily for specialist skills beyond the capabilities of in-house staff, rather than an overflow from the in-house functions of organisations. This explains the dominance of expert, niche market activities of teleworking businesses and the relatively high incomes of workers in both study areas. Certainly, the most important attributes for successful teleworking appear to be expertise, reputations and networks of client contacts developed within former employment, usually within large, mainly urban-based organisations. Such companies have acted as important incubators to small firm growth, often providing encouragement to the establishment of the business. This influence is reflected in the concentration of teleworking businesses in the same sector as workers' previous employment. Indeed, the evidence from the research demonstrates the importance of 'insider knowledge' in facilitating rural-based telework, as markets and reputations are already established in predominantly urban centres prior to commencing a telework operation in the countryside. Clearly, therefore, urban areas are important seedbeds of telework activity and the growth of telework in the countryside appears largely determined by the residential preferences of potential and actual teleworkers. Indigenous rural telework activity (for example, through telecottages), on the other hand, appears constrained to providing routine, low skill services to predominantly local markets.

While developments in ICT have theoretically enabled particular information-based services to be provided remotely, such spatial independence may be moderated by the requirement of these businesses to interact closely with clients, restricting trade to local or regional markets. Despite the evidence of a considerable interregional and international exchange of work, regional influences were still apparent in the client sectors served by teleworkers, for example public organisations and SMEs in Wales and large private organisations in the South East. Regional patterns of demand also influenced the degrees and types of specialisation within the supply of rural telework. This suggests that, while teleworkers in Wales may have to be more diverse and adaptable in the markets they serve, teleworkers in the South East can be more specialist due to their proximity to concentrations of diverse economic activities in the region generally. This also means that telework activities in this area are generally easier to establish and sustain.

However, it emerged that concentrations of regional clients do not reflect a requirement for close proximity between the supply of, and demand for, telework. Rather, the distribution of clients has been linked mainly to the residential characteristics of teleworkers interviewed, in that most lived close to where they had previously worked, and as such where their main markets were located. Furthermore, certain types of teleworkers in both study areas had concentrations of clients in very remote markets. These tended to be those who had relocated into the study areas away from their established markets and also those in particular market sectors, for example, translation, which had been specifically structured in order to deal with teleworking translators located across the world. Indeed, the results from the study do suggest that the nature of services traded and the residential dynamics of teleworkers largely determine their distance from markets and the levels of remote and direct communication sustained with clients. As a result, in terms of the characteristics of telework, differences within the case study areas were often as great as the differences between them, making general comparisons between the two areas problematic.

While the use of ICT and more traditional forms of remote communication greatly facilitated the remote working situation, there was still a need for direct, face to face interaction between teleworkers and clients. This was particularly evident for bespoke and specialist functions such as consultancy and market research, where services traded were often in-tangible, and direct interaction enabled teleworkers to determine and satisfy the demands of clients more effectively. For services such as translation and journalism on the other hand, where minimal input was required from clients, the need for direct interaction was considerably less. While the demand for face to face contact in undertaking work has often been perceived as a considerable inhibitor to the development of telework, the requirement for face to face interaction with clients did not appear to constrain, or be constrained by, the location of teleworkers or distances from markets. Certainly, both teleworkers and organisations considered the financial and physical inconveniences of direct interaction an accepted part of the situation and ultimately necessary if organisations were to gain access to particular areas of expertise, and if workers wanted to live and work at home in the countryside.

The premium placed upon the reputation of teleworkers by organisations highlighted the closed system of teleworker recruitment adopted by them. This appeared to be linked to the insecurities of dealing with teleworkers who had no institutional back up but whose costs were lower than larger, more established organisations. Teleworkers also placed a premium on reputation and particularly the requirement for more informal face to face contact to sustain and establish reputations and new clients. Whilst teleworkers engaged in national and international markets, particularly those in the Wales study area, were less able to interact informally with contacts, it was evident that the situation was presently not having a detrimental impact on their business. However, these effects may, over time, manifest a decrease in work loads.

Certain teleworkers, particularly within the Wales study area, were conscious of how their clients perceived their location as remote and culturally distinct and their working environment as unprofessional. In reality, however, organisations appeared more concerned with acquiring the skills of workers than with their location or working environment. Nonetheless, these negative feelings were often overcome through careful management of the home office environment and through the use of technology to disguise their location. However, it is apparent that until teleworkers feel that rural telework is, in the eyes of clients, an accepted and satisfactory way of working, they may feel beholden to tie themselves to their home office or feel unable, if they so desired, to move to a more rural location.

Despite telecottages being portrayed as important social and technological arenas of interaction for home-based teleworkers, they have not been key elements in the day to day operations of established teleworkers. The low costs of technology, minimal overheads of homeworking and a lack of social isolation have meant that teleworkers are more likely to establish their businesses at home. Furthermore, close knit networks of client contacts, colleagues and other self-employed teleworkers, developed through local and non-local business clubs and organisations, appear to provide adequate social and technological support for teleworkers.

10.3 The development of teleworking in the British countryside

Much of the literature on telework, and changing work practices generally, has pointed to economic restructuring and the desire of companies to achieve increased organisational flexibility as causing the demand for more flexible working practices, such as telework. However, the research revealed that, although organisations clearly benefited from the flexibility engendered through the use of teleworkers, the causes of an increased adoption of telework reflected a variety of forces rather than any single factor.

Whilst organisational restructuring and externalisation should not be underestimated in terms of influencing the increased demand for sub-contracting, and therefore telework, it was also evident that the use of independent sub-contractors had been undertaken by organisations since the early 1970s, possibly before periods of rationalisation had taken place. Furthermore, it was apparent that the supply of telework in this study was influenced less by redundancy and externalisation and more by the aspirations of individuals for self-direction and spatial, residential and temporal flexibility that could be realised through teleworking.

Although decisions to telework have often been linked to a desire to work at home, the motivations of individuals to telework related more closely to aspirations of self-employment than to homeworking. It was merely coincidental that a home-based office was cheaper and more convenient than renting an office space outside of the home. The lack of conventional employment opportunities (both in terms of availability and suitability) in the local area also influenced the supply of telework, particularly within Wales where opportunities for successful income generation appeared restricted to self-employment. The supply of telework was also heavily influenced by previous reputations and networks of client contacts developed within previous employment. These attributes were highly transferable and not closely tied to organisations and, coupled with low barriers to entry, enabled workers to leave established firms and set up on their own with comparative ease.

It would therefore appear that the factors underpinning telework generally are as much linked to organisations pursuing more flexible labour use strategies as skilled individuals wishing to work independently of established organisations. Thus, while the literature on changing work patterns has often associated the initiation of the demand of these working practices with the changing requirements of organisations, individual workers have exerted considerable influence on how organisations gain access to their expertise. Ultimately, however, it can be inferred that organisational restructuring, as a consequence of the so called Fordist crisis of the 1970s, has been of significant historical importance in facilitating a demand orientated culture of sub-contracting more generally. Supply-side factors, on the other hand, have been more important in explaining the growth of self-employed telework more specifically in recent years.

As for the factors underpinning the development of teleworking in the countryside, the telework literature has pointed to the role of various agencies as important facilitators of rural telework - acting as links between the supply of, and demand for, such working practices. The research demonstrated that agencies in both areas have been active in establishing telework facilitation strategies, although such activity in the Wales study area has been significantly greater than in the South East study area. This can be linked to the considerable financial support given to telework projects from the European Union due to the Objective 5b designation given to these areas of rural Wales. The provision of access to workspace, ICT, training and advice via telecottages has been the principal and often only response of agencies in attempting to facilitate telework within the study areas. However, public agencies, through the development of telecottages, have not played any significant role in facilitating rural telework. Successful teleworkers have tended to establish largely urban-based markets, through contacts developed within former employment, prior to commencing a teleworking business in the rural study areas. Therefore, establishing and maintaining telework through supply and demand interaction has depended less upon the use of ICT, and more upon intimate knowledge of, and established relationships within, predominantly urban-based markets. Indeed, it has been non-technological constraints, such as accessing remote urban markets, the development of reputations and establishing a demand for routine functions, which have hindered the development of telecottages and also of teleworkers providing routine functions not closely linked to previous employment. While projects such as TELEMART have attempted to redress these non-technological aspects in order to develop indigenous telework, other facilitation strategies must consider the organisational, sectoral and skill aspects of these working practices in addition to the role of technology in telework.

While many teleworkers were already living in the study areas prior to starting a business, others had relocated into the study areas from largely urban centres after becoming a teleworker. The motivations behind the in-migration of these individuals were influenced primarily by lifestyle aspirations and the realisation that their business operation was neither spatially dependent upon the location of their markets nor constrained by the decisions or perceptions of their clients. There was also wider awareness of the spatial flexibilities of telework, and several teleworkers had considered relocating to more desirable locations in the future. It was therefore evident that the existence of telework in rural areas did not appear to be linked to any geographically determined labour use strategy employed by organisations.

Telework appears to be a permanent rather than temporary response to the changing requirements of organisations and workers. Indeed, many of the reasons given by organisations and teleworkers for initially adopting such new work practices were similarly given in respect to maintaining the status quo. Many of the advantages accrued to organisations by using teleworkers related to notions of post-Fordist forms of organisational flexibility and the ability to expand and contract in line with fluctuating markets through the use of competitive outsiders rather than more expensive in-house sources. The use of teleworkers rather than larger enterprises was linked primarily to cost, although additional advantages related to being able to deal with a small scale and flexible operation rather than a larger and organisationally more rigid enterprise.

For individual teleworkers, flexibility, control, independence and the general experience of 'being one's own boss' were given as dominant advantages of their situation. While these benefits were accompanied by concerns about insecurity, engendered by the short-term nature of sub-contracting, these feelings were predominantly psychological. The experience of homeworking was generally positive, although problems with the inability to switch off from work were apparent. These feelings were, however, as much to do with the responsibilities and pressures of running one's own business, as with working at home. Nevertheless, these problems were significantly reduced when workspaces had been established outside of the immediate home-space such as in garages or log cabins in the garden.

While social isolation has been regarded as the greatest inhibiting factor to the widespread adoption of telework this has not been a significant problem for teleworkers in this study. This characteristic can be linked to the existence of close knit networks of colleagues and client contacts sustained through verbal interaction via the telephone and occasional face to face meetings. In addition, integration into networks of other self-employed workers through local and more distant organisations had increased levels of social interaction amongst such workers, and in some cases led to collaboration on contracts and the development of 'virtual' companies. This helped reduce feelings of professional isolation and offered new opportunities for skill sharing and development for teleworkers. Certainly, the generally favourable conditions under which most of the teleworkers in the study operated would suggest that, rather than being a peripheral component of the workforce whose working conditions were determined by the demands of organisations, they were valued individuals with specific skills which were vital to the successful operations of larger organisations.

In more general terms, the evidence from this study tends to point to self-employed telework as a social and economic counter-culture. From the organisational perspective, it reflects emergent shifts towards post-Fordism, increased flexibility in the capitalist mode of production and, perhaps more significantly, flexible specialisation. These new organisational forms have been seen to involve large numbers of small but technologically advanced firms, operating within a network of similar enterprises but linked, through a relationship of reciprocity, to larger organisations integrated into national and international markets (Piore and Sabel, 1984). These systems have replaced the hierarchical multi-functional and multi-locational enterprises which characterised Fordist systems of production in the post war period. At the same time, telework has reflected a shift in the work and non-work aspirations of individual workers. Such aspirations appear rooted in a desire of certain groups to escape the size and corporate nature of organisations and to achieve flexibility, not only in their work, but also in their home lives. It has also reflected, in some cases, a reaction to urban living and an inherent desire to live idyllic lifestyles in the countryside.

10.4 Implications of the research for rural policy and planning

In addition to offering an insight into the various policy initiatives regarding the facilitation of telework in rural areas, the findings from the research have a number of implications for telework, and wider, areas of rural policy. It has already been noted that, to date, agencies have played a limited role in facilitating telework in the study areas, primarily because of their pre-occupation with technology as the enabling factor, and their failure to consider the non-technological aspects of telework development. These problems have been compounded by the funding priorities of certain bodies, for example the European Union, which have meant that telecottages and more specifically techno-centred strategies have been the predominant and often only policy seeking to develop telework in rural areas. Clearly, agencies and policy makers need to reformulate their conception of telework on the basis of empirical research, such as that presented in this study, if they are to reap the perceived economic and social benefits of these new work practices for rural areas. Ultimately, they must recognise that the ability to telework in the countryside is constrained less by the ability to work remotely through the use of ICT, and more by the acquisition of particular marketable skills and established networks of client contacts located in distant, predominantly urban markets.

However, it is recognised that continued efforts of agencies to 'wire up' the countryside, the marketing of rural areas as suitable telework spaces and the development of more advanced technologies such as digital cable networks and video conferencing, may serve to decrease the problems (both perceived and actual) of living and working remotely. Indeed, the research has indicated that telework has facilitated, and may further facilitate, the increased in-movement of professional service classes into rural areas.   However, certain commentators have questioned whether encouraging the development of telework is beneficial to rural areas and whether an in-movement of professional teleworkers may contribute to, or hinder, the social and economic well-being of such areas. Rising house prices, increased cultural conflict and social polarisation may be a consequence of such trends. However, the evidence from this study does suggest that teleworkers are contributing to their local economy and society. For instance the majority of teleworkers in this study had clients outside the local area, which meant that income was being brought into, rather than recycled within, the area. In addition, this income was spent locally as teleworkers' home and work lives were firmly routed in the local community rather than being spatially fragmented, as with commuters. This also gave rise to greater community participation on the part of teleworkers and their families in terms of membership to local clubs, societies and community groups. However, given the contrasting views of commentators with regards to such trends (see for example Toffler, 1980 and O'Siochru, 1991), there remains a need for a more systematic evaluation of the economic and social implications for, and multiplier effects on, rural economies and societies that such changes may engender.

Another important finding was that, despite the success of the teleworking businesses, and the general desire of teleworkers to continue working in this way, there was considerable evidence to suggest that they would not grow into large businesses. Many of the factors that led individuals to set up on their own, such as autonomy and independence, were the same factors that motivated them to keep the business small. These findings are in contrast to suggestions by other researchers that such aspirations are likely to decrease after the initial conception of the business, when workers become aware of its growth potential (Hakim, 1989). This evidence also contradicts the 'acorns into oak trees' hypothesis which appears to underpin certain economic development policies of local development agencies such as TECs. However, collaboration with other teleworkers has meant that businesses have been expanding through networks of sub-contractors. As such, normative notions of expansion, often employed in the literature on business growth, do not take into consideration actual, and the potential for, employment growth through sub-contracting to other self-employed individuals.

Given the importance of small business clubs and professional bodies as important arenas of teleworker interaction, there exists scope in rural areas for the provision of support, maybe through TECs and local development agencies, to promote and facilitate inter-firm networking. This may encourage the establishment of networks of sub-contracting relationships between firms located in rural areas and also overseas, engendering the expansion of telework activities, improving the social environment of such workers and perhaps leading to a more even regional distribution of employment opportunities. Specific policy could focus upon the establishment of a register of teleworkers and the promotion of small business clubs, maybe via telecottages, which could be integrated into a larger European network of teleworkers. Such activities may also increase the demand for the services of teleworkers providing routine functions such as word processing, as the administration of multi-teleworker collaboration becomes more complex. As a result, employment opportunities for local indigenous groups, who may not have the skills of more professional teleworkers, will be greatly enhanced.

As well as contributing to the society and economy of rural areas, trends towards a de-urbanisation of employment and the restructuring of the workplace, as highlighted in this research, have implications for the environment and transport in rural areas. For instance, the development of telework may clearly lead to a reduction in commuting. However, it is also evident such trends may be tempered by other factors. For example, it emerged that the shift into self-employed telework was accompanied by the acquisition of more remote clients and consequently, while journeys to visit clients were less regular than daily commuting, these journeys were often considerably longer involving car, and sometimes air-based forms of transport. There was also a small amount of evidence to suggest that a reduction in commuting in conjunction with the temporal flexibility of telework actually generated a latent demand for travel.

10.5 Possible areas for future research activity

Many policy documents have speculated about the nature and extent of telework. However, there presently exists no reliable statistics on the degree of teleworking in the UK, let alone in rural areas. Considering the ever-increasing interest in telework and the debates concerning its development, there is an immediate requirement to improve sources of statistical information so that a more detailed impression of the extent of different forms of telework in the UK can be generated. To illustrate, it is presently impossible to cross tabulate data on homeworking with self-employment and occupation from published sources of the OPCS census surveys, despite such data being available separately.

This book has been limited to an exploration of a small number of situations in two specific rural settings. Inevitably therefore, there have been certain aspects of rural telework which this book has only touched upon. Some possible areas for future study have already been highlighted, including an exploration of the social and economic multiplier effects of telework on rural communities. Attention could also be given to a longitudinal investigation of telework, in order to reveal whether the relocation of teleworkers into the countryside may have detrimental impacts on the success of their businesses. Certainly, as most of the teleworking businesses studied had only been recently established, such an investigation may also reveal more systematically the degree to which telework represents a temporary solution to the social and economic needs of teleworkers and organisations or constitutes a permanent shift in work patterns.

It emerged from this research project that the acquisition and use of ICT was an important facilitative factor in the development of telework. Although these technologies were primarily utilised by teleworkers for sending documents, future research may focus on the development of more advanced technologies, such as video conferencing and interactive document processing, and the ways in which they could transform patterns of remote working by reducing the need for both formal and informal direct face to face interaction. In addition, an analysis of present telecommunications policy is required in order to establish whether it is conducive to the provision of universal (i.e. rural and urban) digital telecommunications networks, for example cable, which will be critical in supporting the widespread adoption of these new services.

While previous research has tended to generalise across different forms of telework, this project has focused on one contractually and spatially distinct type. However, it is acknowledged that there exists many other types which remain under researched which may exhibit considerably different characteristics. Telework in this study has been considered beneficial by both organisations and individuals undertaking these new work practices. Additional research could explore the extent to which other forms of telework, for example, employed telework, exhibit similarly positive motivations and experiences, or whether they have been involuntarily imposed, perhaps reducing rather than enhancing the quality of working conditions.

It also emerged from the research that the nature of the teleworking business greatly influenced the characteristics of the remote working situation. Different markets and services were characterised by different types of contracts, varying levels of reliance on remote and direct client interaction and, as such, determined the spatial independence of teleworkers. Thus, while there is a need to focus upon spatially and distinct forms of telework, there is also a requirement for future studies to concentrate upon the development of telework within particular market sectors. Furthermore, this study has not considered teleworking in an urban context and future studies may explore the differences between urban and rural teleworkers in terms of patterns of direct and remote interaction and security of work flow. Certainly, the importance of urban centres as main seedbeds of telework growth was clearly evident in the study.

It has already been acknowledged that the use of snowballing as the main selection strategy of teleworkers studied may have given rise to a bias towards successful in-migrant teleworkers in contrast to indigenous teleworkers who may have generated their work via telecottages. In mitigation, however, there was strong evidence to suggest that indigenous telework activity was undeveloped and that telecottages played only a limited role in the operations of successful teleworkers. Nonetheless, given the optimistic visions of certain commentators of the annihilation of the spatial disadvantages of rural areas through telework, further research is clearly required to establish the degree to which indigenous rural dwellers may be able to use telework in order to integrate into mainstream, urban-based employment. Presently, however, it appears that rural teleworking is likely to be the exclusive domain of those individuals with skills developed within, and relevant to, the urban-centred information economy.

Bibliography

Acorn Televillages (undated) *Acorn Televillages, Communities that Work,* Acorn Televillages

Albrechtsen, A. (1991) *Integrated Rural Development in Europe and the Third World,* Paper presented at the University of Wales Aberystwyth, November 29th 1991

Allen, S. and Wolkowitz, C. (1987) *Homeworking: Myths and Realities,* Macmillan, Basingstoke

Applegarth, J. (1985) 'The other side: What's good about the home office?' in Forester, T. (ed.) *The Information Technology Revolution,* Basil Blackwell, Oxford

Atkinson, J. (1984) *Flexibility, Uncertainty and Manpower Management,* Institute of Manpower Studies, Report 89, University of Sussex, Falmer

Atkinson, J. and Meager, N. (1986) *Changing Working Patterns: How Companies Achieve Flexibility to Meet New Needs,* NEDO, London

Bannister, N. (1993) Cottage industry looks up, *The Guardian,* 3rd April, p. 4

Batt, S. (1992) 'Teleworking in Devon' in Denbigh, A. (ed.) *Telecottages - The UK Experience,* Report of the 1992 ACRE seminar, pp. 7-12, ACRE, Cirencester

Bell, D. (1974) *The Coming of Post-industrial Society: A Venture in Social Forecasting,* Peregrine, Harmondsworth

Berry, B.J.L. (ed.) (1976) *Urbanisation and Counterurbanisation,* Sage, Beverley Hills

Bevan, J., Clark, G., Banerji, N. and Hakim, C. (1989) *Barriers to Business Start Up: A Study of the Flow into and out of Self-employment,* Research Paper 71, Department of Employment, Sheffield.

Beyers, W.B. and Alvine, M.J. (1985) Export services in post-industrial society, *Papers of the Regional Science Association,* 57, pp. 33-45

Bibby, A. (1995) *Teleworking - Thirteen Journeys to the Future of Work,* Calouste Gulbenkian Foundation, London

Birley, S. and Westhead, P. (1994) New producer businesses: Are they any different from new manufacturing ventures?, *Service Industries Journal,* Vol. 14, No. 4, pp. 455-481

Blanc, G. (1988) 'Autonomy, telework and emerging cultural values' in Korte, W.B., Robinson, S., and Steinle, W.J. (eds.) *Telework: Present Situation and Future Development of a New form of Work Organisation*, Elsevier Science, North Holland

Bogenhold, D. and Staber, U. (1991) The Decline and Rise of Self-employment, *Work, Employment and Society*, Vol. 5, No. 2, pp. 223-239

Bogenhold, D. and Staber, U. (1993) self-employment dynamics: A Reply to Meager, *Work, Employment and Society*, Vol. 7, No. 3, pp.465-472

Bolton, N. and Chalkely, B. (1990) The rural population turnaround: A case study of North Devon, *Journal of Rural Studies*, Vol. 6. No. 1 pp. 29-43

Boyer, R. (1988) *The Search for Labour Market Flexibility: The European Economies in Transition*, Clarendon Press, Oxford

Bradley, T. and Lowe, P. (eds.) (1984) *Locality and Rurality*, Geo Books, Norwich

Bright, R. (1987) *Small Businesses and Nine Years of Enterprise Culture*, Conservative Party, London

Britton, S (1990) The role of services in production, *Progress in Human Geography*, 14, pp. 529-46

Brooks, S. (1991) 'The lessons learned in 18 months of operation' in Denbigh, A (ed.) *Telecottages Today, Report of the May 1991 Seminar*, ACRE, Cirencester

Bryson, J., Keeble, D. and Wood, P. (1993) The creation, location and growth of small business service firms in the United Kingdom, *Service Industries Journal*, Vol. 13, No. 2, pp. 118-131

Burgess, J. (1992) 'The art of interviewing' in Rogers, A., Viles, H., and Goudie, A. (eds.) *The Students Companion to Geography*, Blackwell, Oxford

Burrows, R. (1991) 'Entrepreneurship, petty capitalism and economic restructuring of Britain' in Burrows, R. and Curran, J. (eds.) *Deciphering the Enterprise Culture: Entrepreneurship, Petty Capitalism and the Restructuring of Britain*, Routledge, London

Burrows, R. (1991) 'Socio-economic anatomy of the British petty bourgeoisie: a multivariate analysis' in Burrows, R. and Curran, J. (eds.) *Deciphering the Enterprise Culture: Entrepreneurship, Petty Capitalism and the Restructuring of Britain*, Routledge, London

Burrows, R. and Curran, J. (1989) Sociological research on service sector small businesses: Some conceptual considerations, *Work Employment and Society*, Vol. 3, No. 4, pp. 527-539

Campbell, M. and Daly, M. (1992) Self-employment into the 1990s, *Employment Gazette*, June 1992, pp. 269-291

Carter, S. and Cannon, T. (1988) Women in business, *Employment Gazette* Vol. 96, No. 10, pp. 565-571

Casey, B. and Creigh, S. (1988) Self-employment in Great Britain: Its definition in the Labour Force Survey in Tax and Social Security Law and in Labour Law, *Work Employment and Society*, Vol. 2, No. 3, pp. 381-391

Champion, A. (1994) Population change and migration in Britain since 1981: Evidence for continuing deconcentration, *Environment and Planning A*, Vol. 26, pp. 1501-1520

Christensen, K. (1989) 'Home-based clerical work: No simple truth, no single reality' in Boris, E. and Daniels, C. R. (eds.) *Homework: Historical and contemporary perspectives on paid labour at home*, University of Illinois Press, Chicago

Claff, G. (1992) 'The Eccles House Farm Telebusiness Centre' in Denbigh, A. (ed.) *Telecottages - the UK Experience, Report of the 1992 ACRE Seminar*, ACRE, Cirencester

Cloke, P. (1985) Counterurbanisation: a rural perspective, *Geography*, 70, pp. 13-23

Cloke, P., Goodwin, M. and Milbourne, P. (1997) *Rural Wales: Community and Marginalisation*, University of Wales Press, Cardiff

Cloke, P., Milbourne, P. and Thomas C. (1994) *Lifestyles in Rural England*, Rural Development Commission Rural Research Series, Rural Research Report No. 18, Rural Development Commission, London

Cloke, P., Philo, C., and Sadler, D. (1991) *Approaching Human Geography: An Introduction to Contemporary Theoretical Debates*, PCP, London

Coffey, W.J. and Bailley, A.S. (1991) Producer services and flexible production: An exploratory analysis, *Growth and Change*, 22 (4), pp. 95-117

Cohn, M. (1992) Tele tale signs, *The Guardian*, November 6th, p. 27

Coles, M. (1992) High tech cottage industry, *Sunday Telegraph*, November 5th, p. 53

Connolly, S. (1988) Homeworking through technology: Opportunities and opposition - Part two, *Industrial Management and Data Systems* (Bradford), Vol. 88, pp. 7-12

Consortium of Rural Training and Enterprise Councils (CORT) (1991) *Report on Research Into Innovative Practice Amongst Member TECs* - October - November 1991, CORT

Cooper, A.C. (1981) Strategic management new ventures and small business, *Long Range Planning*, Vol. 14, pp. 39-45

Cross, T.B. and Raizman, M. (1986) *Telecommuting: The Future Technology of Work*, Dow Jones-Irwin, Homewood

Crossan, G. and Burton, P.F. (1993) Teleworking stereotypes: A case study, *Journal of Information Science*, Vol. 19, pp. 349-362

Cullen, I.G. (1976) Human geography, regional science and the study of individual behaviour, *Environment Planning A*, Vol. 8, pp. 397-410

Cullen, K., Moran, R., Kenny, S. and Murray, B. (1989) *Teleworking Applications and Potential - TEAPOT: A Feasibility Study of Home-based and Centre Based Telework for People with Physical Disabilities*, Work Research Centre, National Rehabilitation Board, Dublin

CURDS (Centre for Urban and Regional Development Studies) (1995) CURDS Telecottage Survey quoted in Gillespie, A., Richardson, R. and Cornford, J. (1995) *Review of Telework: Implications for Public Policy: Prepared for the Parliamentary Office of Science and Technology,* CURDS, Newcastle

Curran, J. (1990) Rethinking economic structure: Exploring the role of the small firm and self-employment in the British economy, *Work Employment and Society*, additional special issue, May

Curran, J., Stanworth, J. and Watkins, D. (eds.) (1986) *The Survival of the Small Firm, Vol. 2*, Gower, Aldershot

Curson, C. (ed.) (1986) *Flexible Patterns of Work*, Institute of Personnel Management, London

Dahlman, C. (1979) The problem of externality, *The Journal of Law and Economics*, 22, pp. 141-162

Dale, A. (1986) Social class and the self-employed, *Sociology*, Vol. 20, No. 3 pp. 430-434

Dale, A. (1990) 'Self-employment and entrepreneurship: Notes of two problematic concepts' in Burrows, R. and Curran, J. (eds.) *Deciphering the Enterprise Culture: Entrepreneurship, Petty Capitalism and the Restructuring of Britain*, Routledge, London

Daniels, P. (1986) 'Producer services and the post-industrial space economy' in Martin, R. and Rowthorn, B. (eds.) *The Geography of De-Industrialisation*, Macmillan Education, London

Day, G. (1989) 'A million on the move?': Population change and rural Wales, *Contemporary Wales*, pp. 137-159

Denbigh, A. (1991) 'The UK telecottage scene' in Denbigh, A. (ed.) *Telecottages Today, Report of the May 1991 Seminar*, ACRE, Cirencester

Denbigh, A. (1992)'The UK Telecottage - Growth and Potential' in Denbigh, A. (ed.) *Telecottages - the UK Experience, Report of the 1992 Seminar*, ACRE, Cirencester

Dey, I. (1994) *Qualitative Data Analysis: A User Friendly Guide for Social Scientists*, Routledge, London

Di Martino, V. and Wirth, L. (1990) Telework: A way of working and living, *International Labour Review*, Vol. 129, No. 5 pp. 529-554

Diebold Group (1981) *Office Work in the Home: Scenarios and Prospects for the 1980s*, Diebold Group, New York

Dobbs, A. (1990) 'Telecottages in the United Kingdom' in Watkins (ed.) *Teleworking and Telecottages*: *Seminar Report*, 17th October 1989, ACRE, Cirencester

Duncan, J. (1985) Individual action and political power; A structuration perspective in Johnston, R.J. (ed.) *The Future of Geography*, Methuen, London

EDAW Ltd. (1996) *Telecottages Wales, Final Report*, July 1996, EDAW Ltd.

Edwards, P. and Edwards, S. (1985) *Working From Home: Everything you Need to Know About Living and Working under the Same Roof*, Houghton Miffin

Eyles, J. and Smith, D. (1988) *Qualitative Methods in Human Geography*, Polity Press, Cambridge

Farwell, D.C. and Farwell B. M. 'Telecommuting' in Kent, A. (ed.) *Encyclopaedia of Library and Information Science*, 43 (supplement 8), Marcel Dekker, New York

Finch, S. (1991) 'The commercial prospects for telecottages' in Denbigh, A. (ed.) *Telecottages Today: Report of the May 1991 Seminar*, ACRE, Cirencester

Fothergill, A. (1994) *Telework: The Sociological Implications for Individuals and their Families*, paper presented at the BSA Annual Conference: Sexualities in Social Context, University of Central Lancashire

Fritz, M.E.W., Kunihiko, H. and Narasimhan, S. (1995) Toward a telework taxonomy and test for suitability: A synthesis of the literature, *Group Discussion and Negotiation*, 4, pp. 311-332

Giddens, A. (1976) *New Rules of Sociological Method*, Hutchinson, London

Giddens, A. (1984) *The Constitution of Society*, Polity, Oxford

Gilbert, N., Burrows, R. and Pollert, A. (eds.) (1992) *Fordism and Flexibility - Divisions and Change*, Explorations in Sociology 41, British Sociological Association, Macmillan Press, London

Gill, R. and Pratt, A.C. (1992) *Focus Groups and Fine Grained Textual Analysis as a Method of Labour Market Analysis*, Paper Presented at the RESSG Annual Conference, 11-13th December, Hull University

Gillespie, A. and Hepworth, M (eds.) *Telecommunication and Regional Development in the Information Economy - A Policy Perspective*, Economic and Social Research Council, London

Gillespie, A. and Richardson, R. (1994) *Advanced Communications and Regional Development: The Highlands and Islands of Scotland*, Mimeo

Gillespie, A., Richardson, R. and Cornford, J. (1995) *Review of Telework: Implications for Public Policy: Prepared for the Parliamentary Office of Science and Technology*, CURDS, Newcastle

Glaser, B.G. and Strauss, A.L. (1967) *The Discovery of Grounded Theory*, Aldine, New York

Gold, J.R. and Goodey, B. (1984) Behavioural and perceptual geography: criticisms and responses, *Progress in Human Geography*, Vol 8, pp. 544-550

Goodwin, M., Cloke, P. and Milbourne, P. (1995) Regulation theory and rural research - Theorising contemporary rural change, *Environment and Planning A*, Vol. 27, pp. 1245-1260

Gordon, G. E. (1988) 'The dilemma of telework: Technology Vs tradition' in Korte, W.B., Robinson, S. and Steinle, W.J. (eds.) *Telework: Present Situation and Future Development of a New Form of Work Organisation*, Elsevier Science Publishers, North Holland

Gordon, G.E. and Kelly, M.M. (1986) *Telecommuting: How to Make it Work for You and Your Company*, Prentice Hall

Granger, B., Stanworth, J. and Stanworth, C. (1995) Self-employment dynamics: The case of unemployment push in UK book publishing, *Work, Employment and Society*, Vol. 9, No.3, pp. 499-516

Gray, M. Hodson, N. and Gordon, G. (1993) *Teleworking Explained*, Wiley, Chichester

Guelke, L. (1974) An idealist alternative in human geography, *Annals, Association of American Geographers*, Vol. 64, pp. 163-202

Haddon, L. and Silverstone, R. (1993) *Teleworking in the 1990's - A View From the Home*, SPRU CICT Report Series No. 10, SPRU, Sussex

Hakim, C. (1988) Self-employment in Britain: Recent trends and current issues, *Work, Employment and Society*, Vol. 2. No. 4, pp. 421-450

Hakim, C. (1989) New recruits to self-employment in the 1980s, *Employment Gazette*, June, pp. 286-297

Halfacree, K. (1995) Talking about rurality: Social representations of the rural as expressed by residents of six parishes, *Journal of Rural Studies*, 11, pp. 1-20

Handy, C. (1984) *The Future of Work*, Basil Blackwell, Oxford

Handy, C. (1995) *Beyond Uncertainty - The Changing World of Organisations*, Hutchinson, London

Harvey, D. (1989) *The Condition of Post Modernity*, Basil Blackwell, Oxford

Henderson, D. (1994) *Advanced Telecommunications, Remote Working and European Regional Development*, paper given at ISDN User Forum, Stockholm, April 1994

Henley Centre for Forecasting (1989) *Tomorrow's Workplace - Harnessing the Challenge of Teleworking*, Henley Centre for Forecasting, London

Heritage, J. (1984) *Garfunkel and Ethnomethodology*, Polity, Cambridge

High Level Group on the Information Society (1994) *Europe and the Global Information Society, Recommendations to the European Council (The Bangerman Report)*, Commission of the European Communities, Brussels

Highlands and Islands Enterprise (undated) *Teleworking in the Highlands and Islands of Scotland: A Place to Spread Your Wings*, Highlands and Islands Enterprise, Inverness

Hitchens, D.M., O'Farrell, P.N. and Conway, C. (1994) Business service use by manufacturing firms in Mid Wales, *Environment and Planning A*, Vol. 26, pp. 95-106

Huws, U. (1984a) *The New Homeworkers: New Technology and the Changing Location of White Collar Work*, Low Pay Unit, London

Huws, U. (1984b) New Technology Homeworkers, *Employment Gazette*, January 1984, pp. 13-17

Huws, U. (1993) *Teleworking in Britain A Report to the Employment Department*, Research Series No. 18, Employment Department, Sheffield

Huws, U. (1996) *Teleworking: Overview of the Research: A Report to the Department of Transport, Environment, Trade and Industry and Education and Employment*, Analytica, London

Huws, U., Honey, H., and Morris, S. (1996) *Teleworking and Rural Development*, Rural Research Report Number 27, The Rural Development Commission, London

Huws, U., Korte, W. B. and Robinson, S. (1990) *Telework: Towards the Elusive Office*, John Wiley and Sons, Chichester

Illeris, S. (1994) Proximity between service producers and service users, *Tijdschrift voor Economoische en Sociale Geografie*, Vol. 85, No. 4, pp. 294-301

ILO (International Labour Organisation) (1990) *Telework*, International Labour Office Conditions of work Digest, 9, 1

Jenssen, S. and Kolverid, L. (1991) Reasons leading to start up as determinants of survival among Norwegian entrepreneurs, *Proceedings of the Inaugural Global Conference on Entrepreneurship Research*, Imperial College, London

Johnston, P. (1990) 'Applications of information and communication technologies in rural areas of Europe' in Watkins, C. (ed.) *Teleworking and Telecottages, Seminar Report*, ACRE and Centre for Rural Studies, Cirencester

Johnston, R.J. (1983) *Philosophy and Human Geography: An Introduction to Contemporary Approaches*, Edward Arnold, London

Johnston, R.J. (ed.) (1985) *The Future of Geography*, Methuen, London

Johnston, R.J., Gregory, D. and Smith, D.M (eds) (1981) *The Dictionary of Human Geography*, Second Edition, Basil Blackwell, Oxford

Jones, H., Caird, J., Berry, W. and Dewhurst, J. (1985) Peripheral counter-urbanisation: Findings from an integration of census and survey data in Northern Scotland, *Regional Studies*, Vol. 20, pp. 15-26

Judkins, P., West D. and Drew, J. (1986) *Networking in Organisations: The Rank Xerox Experiment*, Aldershot, Gower

Kawakami, S. S. (1983) *Electronic Homework: Problems and Prospects from a Human Resources Perspective*, LIR 494, University of Illinois at Urbana-Champaign

Keeble, D. (1984) The urban-rural manufacturing shift, *Geography*, 69, pp. 163-6

Keeble, D. (1993) 'Small firm creation, innovation and growth' in Curran, J. and Storey, D. (eds.) *Small Firms in Urban and Rural Locations*, Routledge, London

Keeble, D., Bryson, J., and Wood, P. (1991a) Small firms, business service growth and regional development in the United Kingdom: Some empirical findings, *Regional Studies*, Vol. 25.5, pp. 439-457

Keeble, D., Bryson, J., and Wood, P. (1991b) 'Entrepreneurship and flexibility in business services: The rise of small management consultancy and market research firms in the United Kingdom.' in *Proceedings of the Fourteenth United Kingdom Small Firms Policy and Research Conference, Small Enterprise Development: Policy and Practice in Action*, Manchester Business School, Manchester

Keeble, D., Bryson, J. and Wood, P. (1992a) 'Entrepreneurship and flexibility in business services: The rise of small management consultancy and market research firms in the United Kingdom' in Caley, K., Chittenden, E., Chell, E. and Mason, C. (eds.) *Small Enterprise Development: Policy and Practice in Action*, Paul Chapman, London

Keeble, D., Tyler, P., Broom, G. and Lewis, J. (1992b) *Business Success in the Countryside*, London, HMSO

Kelleher, J. (1995) 'New approaches to rural development in the information age: Rural partnerships and the development of telematics applications' in Tavistock Institute, *Review 1994/1995*, Tavistock Institute, London

Kinsman, F. (1986) *The Telecommuters*, Wiley, Chichester

Korte, W.B. (1988) 'Telework - potential, inception, operation and likely future situation' in Korte, W.B., Robinson, S. and Steinle, W.J. (eds.) *Telework: Present Situation and Future Development of a New Form of Work Organisation*, Elsevier Science Publishers, North Holland

Korte, W.B., Kordney, N. and Robinson, S. (1994) *Telework Penetration, Potential and Practice in Europe - Results from Representative Survey Carried out in the TELDET Project*, Empirica, Mimeo

Kugelmass, J. (1995) *Telecommuting : A Managers Guide to Flexible Work Arrangements*, Lexington Books, New York

LeCompte, M.D. and Goetz, J.P. (1982) Problems of reliability and validity in education research, *Review of Educational Research*, 52 (1), pp. 31-60

Leighton, P. (1982) Employment contracts; A choice of relationships, *Employment Gazette*, 90, 10, pp. 433-439.

Lewis, J. (1988) 'Employment matters', in Marshall J. N. (ed.) *Services and Uneven Development*, Oxford University Press, Oxford

Little, J. (1987) 'Gentrification and the influence of local level planning' in Cloke, P. (ed.) *Rural Planning: Policy into Action?* Harper Row, London

Marshall, J. N. (1988) *Services and Uneven Development*, Oxford University Press, Oxford

Martinelli, F. (1991) 'A demand orientated approach to understanding producer services', in Daniels, P. W. and Moulaert, F. (eds.) *The Changing Geography of Advanced Producer Services*, Belhaven Press, London

Maxwell, J. A. (1992) Understanding and validity in qualitative research, *Harvard Educational Review*, 62 (3), pp. 279-300

McGhie, C. (1993) The new ruralists, *Independent on Sunday*, April 4th, pp. 70-73

McHenry, H. (1995) *Understanding the Farmer's View: Perceptions of Changing Agriculture and the Move to Agri-Environmental Policies in Southern Scotland*, Unpublished PhD Thesis, University of Aberdeen

Meager, N. (1990) *Self-employment in the United Kingdom*, IMS Report No. 205, Institute of Manpower Studies, London

Miles, M.B. and Huberman, A.M. (1994) *Qualitative Data Analysis: An Expanded Sourcebook, Second Edition*, Sage Publications, London

Mitchell, J.C. (1983) Case and situational analysis, *Sociological Review*, 31 (2), pp. 187-211

Mitchell, H. (1995) *Plenty of work, not many jobs?* paper presented at the Labour Telematics Conference, 13th January, 1995, Manchester

MITRE (Market Implementation of Teleworking in Rural Environments) (1994), *MITRE Final Report and Implementation Plans*, MITRE Public Report, Home Office Partnership, Cambridge

Moindrot, P. (1991) 'Managing a major teleworking project' in Denbigh, A. (ed.) *Telecottages Today, Report of the May 1991 Seminar*, ACRE, Cirencester

Morley, J. (1994) 'The changing shape of work', in *Telework New Ways to Work: Proceedings of the European Assembly on Teleworking and New Ways of working*, November, 1994, Barleben: Teleport Sachsen-Anhalt, Berlin

Moseley, M.J. (1990) 'Introduction' in Watkins, C. (ed.) *Teleworking and Telecottages, Seminar Report*, ACRE and Centre for Rural Studies, Cirencester

Murray, B. (1995) 'Vital statistics: Results of the telecottage survey', *Teleworker, The Magazine of the Telecottages Association*, No. 7, 1995, pp. 14-16

Murray, R. (1989) 'Fordism and post-Fordism' in Hall, S. and Jacques, M (eds.) *New Times - The Changing Face of Politics in the 1990s*, Lawrence and Wishart, London

Neuman, W.L. (1991) *Social Research Methods*, Allyn and Bacon, Boston

Newby, H. (1985) *Green and Pleasant Land*, Wildwood House, London

Nilles, J. M., Carlson, F.R., Gray, P. and Hanneman, G.J. (1976) *The Telecommunications-Transport Trade-off*, Wiley, New York

Nilles, J. (1985) 'Teleworking from home' in Forester, T. (ed.) *The Information Technology Revolution*, Basil Blackwell, Oxford

Office of Population Census Surveys (1981) *1981 Census Great Britain - National Monitor*, HMSO, London

Office of Population Census Surveys (1991) *1991 Census Great Britain - National Monitor*, HMSO, London

O'Farrel, P.N. (1993) The performance of business service firms in peripheral regions: An international comparison between Scotland and Nova Scotia, *Environment and Planning A*, Vol. 25, pp. 1627-1648

O'Farrell, P.N., Hitchens, D.M. and Moffat, L.A.R. (1993a) Manufacturing demand for business services in a core and peripheral region: Does flexible production imply vertical disintegration of business services?, *Regional Studies*, Vol. 27.5 pp. 385-400

O'Farrell, P.N., Hitchens, D.M. and Moffat, L.A.R. (1993b) The competitiveness of business services and regional development: Evidence from Scotland and the South East of England, *Urban Studies*, Vol. 30, No.10, pp. 1629-1652

O'Farrell, P.N., Hitchens, D.M. and Moffat, L.A.R. (1995) Business service firms in peripheral economies: Scotland and Ireland, *Tijdschrift voor Economoische en Sociale Geografie*, Vol. 86, No. 2, pp. 115-128

Okely, J. (1983) *The Traveller-Gypsies*, Cambridge University Press, Cambridge,

Olson, M. (1981) *Office Work in the Home, Scenarios and Prospects for the 1990's*, Diebold Group, New York

Olson, M. (1988) 'Organisational Barriers to Telework', in Korte, W.B., Robinson, S. and Steinle W.J. (eds.) *Telework: Present Situation and Future Development of a New Form of Work Organisation*, Elsevier Science, North Holland

ORA (Opportunities for Rural Areas) (1993) *Research and Technology Development on Telematic Systems for Rural Areas*, Commission of the European Communities, Brussels

O'Siochru, S (1991) *Europe Connected or Disconnected? Broadband Networks in Less Developed Regions: Regional Evolution Planning for Integrated Rural Communication*, REVOLVE Consortium, Madrid, Fundesco

PATRA (Psychological Aspects of Teleworking in Rural Areas) (undated) *Summary of PATRA's findings*, unpublished, PATRA, Dublin

Patton, M.Q. (1990) *Qualitative Evaluation and Research Methods*, Second Edition, Sage Publications, California

Perry, M. (1992) Flexible production, externalisation and the interpretation of business service growth, *Service Industries Journal*, No. 12, pp. 1-16

Piore, M. and Sabel, C. (1984) *The Second Industrial Divide, Possibilities for Prosperity, New York*, Basic Books

Powell, G. (1992) 'The Wiltshire Telecottage Network' in Denbigh, A. (ed.) *Telecottages - The UK Experience, Report of the 1992 ACRE Seminar*, ACRE, Cirencester

Pratt, J. H. (1983) *Home Teleworking: A study of its Pioneers*, Allied Professionals Education Consulting Service

Pye, R., Tyler, M. and Cartwright, B. (1974) Telecommunicate or travel, *New Scientist*, 12th September

Qvortrup, L. (1994) *Advanced Communication and Regional Development - The Case of Finmark*, Mimeo

Rainee, A. (1992) 'Small firms: Between the enterprise culture and "New Times"' in Burrows, R. and Curran, J. (eds.) *Deciphering the Enterprise Culture: Entrepeneurship, Petty Capitalism and the Restructuring of Britain*, Routledge, London

Rawlins, J. (1989) 'Telework in practice in Rural Areas of Europe' in Watkins, C. (ed.) *Teleworking and Telecottages, Seminar Report*, 17th October 1989, ACRE and Centre for Rural Studies, Cirencester

Richards, L. and Richards, T. (1994) 'From filing cabinet to computer' in Bryman, A. and Burgess, R. (eds.) *Analysing Qualitative Data*, Routledge, London

Ritchie, J. and Spencer, L. (1994) Qualitative data analysis for applied policy research' in Bryman, A. and Burgess, R. (eds.) *Analysing Qualitative Data*, Routledge, London

Robertson, J. (1985) *Future Work: Jobs, Self-employment and Leisure After the Industrial Age*, Gower, Aldershot,

Robson, C. (1993) *Real World Research: A Resource for Social Scientists and Practitioner-Researchers*, Blackwell, Oxford

Rural Development Commission (1990) Teleworking in the countryside, *Rural Focus*, Autumn, pp. 6-7

Sarantakos, S. (1993) *Social Research*, Macmillan Education, Australia

Schiff, F.W. (1983) Flexiplace: Pros and cons, *The Futurist*, June, 1983

Scott, A.J. (1988) *New Industrial Spaces: Flexible Production, Organisation and Regional Development in North America and Western Europe*, Pion, London

Stake, R.E. (1994) 'Case Studies' in Denzin, N. and Lincoln, Y. (eds.) *Handbook of Qualitative Research*, Sage, Thousand Oaks

Stanworth, J. and Stanworth, C. (1991) *Telework: The Human Resource Implications*, Institute of Personnel Management, London

Steinle, W.J. (1988) 'Telework: opening remarks on an open debate', in Korte, W.B., Robinson, S. and Steinle, W.J. (eds.) *Telework: Present Situation and Future Development of a New Form of Work Organisation*, Elsevier Science Publishers, North Holland

Stern, E. and Holti, R. (1986a) *Distance Working - Origins-Diffusion-Prospects*, Commission of the European Communities FAST Programme, Tavistock Institute, Luxembourg

Stern, E. and Holti, R. (1986b) *Distance Working in Rural and Urban Settings*, Tavistock Institute of Human Relations, London

Storey, D., Watson, R. and Wynarczyk, P. (1988) *Fast Growth Small Businesses: Case Studies of 40 Small Firms in North East England*, Research Paper No. 67, Department of Employment, London

Tahar, G. (1980) *The Fringe and Clandestine Labour Market in France, the United Kingdom and Italy*, Commission of the European Communities, Study number 79/42, Brussels

Telecottages Association (1995) *Teleworker: The Magazine of the Telecottages Association*, No. 6

Telecottages Association (1996) *Teleworker: The TCA Magazine*, Vol. 3, No. 2

Telecottages Association (1999) *Teleworker: The Magazine for TCA, TCW and TWI members*, Vol. 6, No. 3

Thrift, N. (1994) *A Phantom State? The Discourses of International Finance*, Lecture given at the Cheltenham and Gloucester College of Higher Education, 4th May, Shaftsbury Hall

Thrift, N. and Leyshon, A. (1992) 'In the wake of money: The city of London and the accumulation of value' in Budd, L. and Whimster, S. (eds.) *Global Finance and Urban Living: A study of Metropolitan Change*, Routledge, London

Toffler, A. (1980) *The Third Wave*, William Morrow, New York

Townsend, A. (1991) 'New forms of employment in rural areas: A national perspective' in Champion, A. and Watkins, C. (eds.) *People in the Countryside: Studies of Social Change in Rural Britain*, PCP, London

Walsh, B. (1992) *A trade union perspective*, proceedings of the Teleworking 1992 Conference, Brighton

Watkins, C. (ed.) (1990) *Teleworking and Telecottages: Papers Presented at the Seminar Organised Jointly by ACRE and CRS at the Royal Agricultural College*, ACRE, Cirencester

Webster, F. and Robins, K. (1979) Mass communications and information technology, *Socialist Register*, pp. 285-313

White, P. (1992), *Untitled Discussion within a Qualitative Methods Workshop*, September, Sheffield University, Sheffield

Wolcott, H. (1994) *Transforming Qualitative Data, Description, Analysis, Interpretation*, Sage, London

Wood, P. (1991) Flexible accumulation and the rise of business services, *Transactions of the Institute of British Geographers*, 16, pp. 160-172

Wood, P., Bryson, J. and Keeble, D. (1993) Regional patterns of small firm development in the business services: Evidence from the United Kingdom, *Environment and Planning A*, Vol. 25, pp. 77-700

Young, Lord (1986) *Enterprise - The Road to Jobs*, London Business School Journal, Vol. 11. No. 1